JAIL SPEAK

OCKERS SLAM!

CK THEM TO MAKE NOISE.

<p. ii blank>

THIS IS WHERE YOU

CAN BE L

PUN

K

THE BATHROOM.

HE URINAL.

LL IT FOR FUN.

CR

ER

JAIL SPEAK

the hyphenate

and throat

SWALLOW PRESS / OHIO UNIVERSITY PRESS

ATHENS, OHIO

SLA

THEM.

THEM, ELBOW THEM ON YOUR WAY PAST.

the guard's locker
on top of the others

OR JUST FLIP IT OVER,
OR,
IF YOU HAVE TIME,
TIE IT TO THE DROP CEILING.

THEN HIDE AND WATCH THAT GUARD SWEAR AND
KICK AND SPIT WHEN HE FINDS IT. FIND
YOUR LOCKER. GEAR UP FOR WORK. PUT ON THE
UNIFORM. LINE UP LIKE A
LIKE A   R   E
ALLOWED, PUT IT AWAY.

BRING A PEN,

GUM'S NOT ALLOWED, EITHER. IT CAN
BE USED TO MAKE KEY IMPRESSIONS.
BRING IT IN ANYWAY. IT DOESN'T
SET OFF THE METAL DETECTOR.

LEAVE THE STAB VEST HANGING
ON THE HOOK. NO ONE'S GOING
TO SHANK YOU.

THEY HAVEN'T YET.

Ben Langston

OUR LOCKER SHUT. BE A MAN. SLAM IT TWICE.

Swallow Press
An imprint of Ohio University Press, Athens, Ohio 45701
ohioswallow.com

Printed in the United States of America
Swallow Press / Ohio University Press books are printed on acid-free paper ⊗ ™

30 29 28 27 26 25 24 23 22 21 20   5 4 3 2 1

Library of Congress Cataloging-in-Publication Data
Names: Langston, Ben, 1976- author.
Title: Jail speak / Ben Langston.
Description: Athens, Ohio : Swallow Press/Ohio Univeristy Press, [2020]
Identifiers: LCCN 2020001361 | ISBN 9780804012256 (trade paperback) | ISBN
  9780804041096 (pdf)
Subjects: LCSH: Langston, Ben, 1976- | State Correctional Institution at
  Rockview (Pa.) | Correctional personnel--Pennsylvania--Biography. |
  Prisoners--Pennsylvania. | Prisons--Pennsylvania.
Classification: LCC HV9475.P42 S725 2020 | DDC 365/.92 [B]--dc23
LC record available at https://lccn.loc.gov/2020001361

For the squad.

The fam.

Life is hard inside.

Because it's life.

This book is honest about jail. So it's graphic.

There is obscenity, racism, sadism, sexism,

rape, suicide, violence, and despair.

I hope the obscenity doesn't offend anyone.

Contents

Preface

I didn't take a jail job to write a book. I didn't even want a jail job. But the TV factory in town turned me down and I was broke and unskilled and mad about being broke and unskilled and the jail was doing something enchanting: it was hiring.

The jail was the State Correctional Institute at Rockview, located in central Pennsylvania, five miles from Penn State University. The area's name: Happy Valley. The jail held two thousand inmates of all security levels and handled the state's executions. It still does. Its purpose and problems are universal to the judicial system. I ended up wearing a corrections officer uniform there for three years.

I call Rockview a "jail" because that's what the guards and inmates called it. The word "prison" is often used for places where guys do sentences of a year or more. "Jails" are typically places where guys do less than a year. So, technically, Rockview would be considered a prison. But really, call it what you want—jail, prison, big house, pokey—it's a place where people are kept against their will. Some of those people make the worst of it. Others, the best. And call me what you want—corrections officer, CO, guard, jailcop—I helped keep people there against their will. For this, the jail rewarded me with paychecks, jail food, and, eventually, a concrete desire to escape.

Jail can be an anywhere, anytime. Bars exist everywhere. The woman who can't leave her abusive husband because she has two lovely freckled children, no job, and no family to take her in, yes, she's in jail. Jail can also be a high-interest loan, a wall between countries, a nightclub for an introvert, or a job that makes you wake up, put on a uniform, and act only according to the uniform. At Rockview, a young inmate had NO REAL FREEDOM tattooed in big block letters down his forearms. Listen to him. He knows what he's tattooing about.

I had advantages in life—born white to educated parents—but chose a restless and distracted life of blue-collar jobs with a term in the army instead of following my parents' examples. And after ten years of unskilled labor I was desperate to work at Rockview. Once hired, my primary occupation became fitting in.

After three weeks at Rockview, I met nineteen-year-old Melvin. He came to jail as an arsonist and burglar charged with eleven felonies and stood tall at four and a half feet. He was the anti-me, with none of life's advantages—born black to a drug-addicted single mother living in poverty—he had to fight and fight and fight. While I tried hard to fit in jail, Melvin was made for it. He never had a chance outside. And despite having an IQ of fifty-eight, the mind of a child, according to paid professionals, he told me once, "You're jealous of me 'cause I don't have to pretend." He was right for that.

The last time I saw Melvin, he had on a suicide-resistant smock and was strapped down to a bunk with five-point restraints. That was my parting image of jail: a tiny man attached to a metal bunk. It showed me how small and helpless people can become inside. Or maybe how massive and abusive. The room smelled like vomit. The scene was hopeless. And I had been the one to strap him down.

At Rockview, the inmates had clear plastic TVs. They were clear for security. You could see the circuit boards, the wiring, the working parts, any contraband, and all the cockroaches breeding inside.

This book is like those TVs.

JAIL SPEAK

Be a Man, Man

SHUT the car door. Look at the jail. Look at the towers, the razor wire, the coal-fired boiler plant, the twelve coats of blue paint on the locker-room door. Take a deep breath. Hold it. Smell the coal dust and iron and dirt and sweat. That's jail. And jail is where dicks are measured. There are thousands in this one. And with all that measuring comes all the testosterone—buckets and buckets.

Smell it as you walk into the locker room. Soak it up. Look at the chew wads on the ceiling, the dried spit on the lockers. Add yours. Get in character. You're a guard. Hear the lockers slam. Kick them to make noise. Here you can be loud. There's no door on the bathroom. Walk in, spit in the urinal. Say *fuck*. Yell it for fun. *Fuck!* Come out and tape the serious guard's locker closed. Then hide. He'll swear and kick and spit when he finds it.

Open your locker. Put on the uniform. It's gray. It's black. It fits like a sack. Wear a watch. No phone allowed. Bring a pen. That's it. No gum either. It can be used to make key impressions. Bring it in anyway. It doesn't set off the metal detector. Leave the stab vest hanging on the hook. No one's going to shank you. They haven't yet. Slam your locker shut. Be a man. Slam it twice.

Walk past the guard with the hairy ass crack standing in only his tighty whities. He's at the exit. Compliment his package. *Nice bulge.* Say it loud.

Stand at the gate. Get jacked because you wait. Kick on the gate. When it buzzes, open it fast, walk in, and hold it for the guard running behind you. Then slam it in his face. Bam. You're a man.

Swear at the time clock. *Fucking clock.* Cry about the fingerprint scan. *Fucking scan.* Throw your keys and belt past the metal detector. Hold up your pants and walk through. When you've made it, watch the next guard start through. Then kick the metal detector. That sets it off. Then run.

Wade through the roll-call room. Hit shoulders, punch kidneys, step on every shiny black boot you see. And twist. When your name is called say HERE like you got a pair. Bitch about the block you get sent to. *Fucking A block.* Bitch about the lieutenants making the schedule, but only after you leave the roll-call room and walk out of earshot, and then go a little farther and then look around to make sure it's clear. Then you can say it. *Fucking white hats.* But not too loud. Or they'll put you at a worse post.

Slam the A block door. It's 6 a.m. Ignore the night shift guards leaving. Call them slugs after they shut the door. *Fucking slugs.* They're soft. They only come out at night.

Smell the block. It's piss. It's smoke. It's piss mist.

Look up at the cells: 250 of them are stacked five stories high. They're back-to-back inside a cage twenty feet away from the outer walls. Know that 500 inmates are up there sleeping. They're about to measure you. Get ready. Grab a radio. It's almost count time. Grab keys and a clipboard. That's it, nothing else. No night stick, no pepper spray. You don't carry all that mess in this jail. You have a made-in-Taiwan whistle on your belt. That's good enough. Whistle if you're shanked.

Get moving. You have to count two ranges. Hurry up. That's two hundred dicks. Get in position. You have one minute until count. Climb the stairs to level 5. You have fifteen seconds. That's a long time to stand. Catch your breath. Rest on the trash can. It's not that dirty. Even if it was, who cares? Not you.

Hear the bell ring. Hear the sergeant say, *Count time* over the PA system. Hear him say, *Lights on, be standing, be visible.* And start counting. Just count heads. Check them off on the sheet. Don't worry about names. You don't care about names. Check off each cell. One, two, check them off. Keep moving. Go fast. Cell 501: one, two. They're mean-mugging you. Mean-mug them back, look tough, or laugh, or stop and stare, that works. Cell 502: one, two. They're smiling at you. Ignore both. Cell 503: one. There's just one. He's pissing. He's looking at you and holding his dick. He's measuring you. Keep your eye contact walking by. Measure him back. Cell 504: one, two. Their backs are turned. Keep moving. Check off cells.

Stop at cell 514. Look at the inmates still sleeping. Look at them not standing, their lights still off. You're a corrections officer. Correct. Say, *Count time.* And wait two seconds. Then yell it. *Count Time!* And wait two more seconds. Then bang your clipboard on the bars as loud as you can until they stop pretending to sleep and stand up and say, "Damn, man, what you doing that for?"

You hear that? He called you a man, man.

Put an extra mark by the sleepers on the count sheet: check and check. You're done counting. Go down and give the block sergeant the count: all. Then find the sleepers' block cards. Know that block cards have mug shots and basic information. Report the jail crime. Write, "Not Standing for Count." While you're at it, draw mustaches on their mugs. Give them black eyes, earrings, dicks in their mouths. If it's a third offense, give them a write-up. Unless you're a member of the hug-a-thug program. Which you're not. Of course. Write them up. Other officers are measuring.

Head back into the cage. Run the ranges. That's your job for two hours. It's not really running. It's slamming. You slam cell doors, you walk, then you slam more cell doors. The guards in the officer station do the opening: twenty-five doors with one button.

Here come the inmates now. It's breakfast, their chance at one serving of protein, fruit, dairy, and carbohydrates. Look at them fly out of the cells. Watch them pile down the stairs. Walk right behind and slam doors. Start at the top, range 5, push the inmates down with slams. Don't take any shit. Don't stop. Just slam. Let them know. Chase them out of the cage. Fucking slam them, man.

Take a break. You're done for now. The inmates are gone for half an hour. Sit on the back stairs. Those stairs are gated off. That way you don't have to deal with the inmate "CO, CO, can I stop by 237?" or "CO, CO, I need my cell opened" when they come back. Just sit and doze until you hear another guard's radio or keys jingling nearby. Then act like you're tying your boots so you don't look lazy.

Stretch when you hear the doors open for the inmates' return. Back to running. Once the inmates step inside, slam their cell doors with a full-on, full-body shove. Rattle the range. Let them know. *Clear the range,* the slams say. *Move.* Don't listen to a word the inmates say. Let the slams answer.

"CO, I've got a dentist's appointment."

Slam.

"CO, I've got a library pass."

Slam.

"CO, I think I broke my leg."

Slam.

Go to the staff dining hall. It's 9 a.m. It smells like meat. Get some. You want two jail hamburgers? Hamburgers for breakfast? Take them. It's steakfast. Take four. They're free. Grab fries. Bump into every guard you walk behind on your way to sit. Wait until they're drinking, then give them a push. Look at the table: sixteen guards grinding burgers. If you sit at another table, they'll give you shit. Don't get a sausage to eat unless you can take the dick jokes. Which you can, man.

Wipe your mouth with your tie. Head back to the block. Walk into the inmates heading to the yard. They're six hundred deep. Punch through the middle. Say, *Make a hole*. Yell, *Make it wide!* It's six hundred against one. This is when they measure you. Hear one yell, "Rent-a-cop." You don't know who it was. You don't care. He wants you to crack. Don't. But say something back. Tell the six hundred, the whole six hundred, to *Rent a dick*.

Walk to the fence by the chapel before going back to A block. Shake the fence with the vibration sensors. Shake it hard. Look up at the camera. Wait until the camera-room operator moves it toward you to check for escapees. Then flip him off—with both hands—and walk away.

Climb the stairs again in the block. This is where you're at until inmates go to lunch. Slam doors. Rest on trash cans. Say *No* to the inmates. Say it over and over. Look at the dust in the air. Know that it's skin cells. Breathe those inmates in. Catch the same loudmouth twice on the wrong range. Tell him that you know him. Tell him that there are 477 inmates on this block and that you know all their names, that you know his name, his number, his cell, his celly, his celly's homies, his celly's homies' honeys. That will shut him up. Yours is bigger. Show him. Slam doors. Slam his. Lock him in.

Listen to Loudmouth still running his loud mouth. He says he can take you, that without the uniform you're nothing, that you're ugly, that you're pathetic, a punk, a pussy on a power trip. He's a cell warrior. He only talks tough once he's behind the bars of his cell. Listen to him talk about your mother, and, because he sees your ring, your wife, too. That's okay. Keep making rounds until you see him doing something in his sink, like dividing up a bag of BBQ chips into bowls. Be patient. Wait until you see him almost done: one bowl for him, one for his celly, and one for his celly's homey's honey. Now go to the back stairs and unlock the door to the maintenance space that runs behind the cells. Walk through the plumbing and dead roaches. Find the back of Loudmouth's cell. Pull the rods that turn the water on to his sink—full fucking blast—to spray the hell out of his chips. Then listen to him him yell, "Fuck! Fuck! Fuck!" Go ahead and laugh. You win.

Brag to the other guard running the ranges. Tell him how you took care of Loudmouth. You can trust the other guard. Maybe. Listen to him laugh. He won't rat. Maybe. He's got your back. Maybe. He's a guard too. He's the same as you for eight hours a day. Maybe. You wear the uniform. It affects you. Let it. You like it. Be a man, you can. Strap on a big one.

If you leave the "I" in the car, there's no "I" to hurt. There's just you. And you're a gate warrior. Inside the gate you're the Institution. Life is simple inside, systematic, stab-resistant. But only if you act right, speak right, sit and eat your fries right.

Relieve the guard working the showers. Hear him say that the burgers are running right through him. Watch the inmates showering, all forty of them. Look at them wearing their boxers. That way they can do laundry—double duty. Some have their T-shirts on, too. It's not allowed, but let it slide, they're just T-shirts. Look at the soap: yellow bricks, state-issued. Smell the steam. Smell the soap. It's industrial, extra strength, extra potent. It numbs your nose.

Stand in the door of the showers. It's almost lunch. Give the inmates a ten-minute warning: *Ten minutes.* Yell it. Hear one of them yell, "Fuck your ten minutes."

Fine. Teach them.

Wait just two minutes, then give them a one-minute warning: *One minute.* Yell it. Then turn off the water right away. Look at them trying to towel their suds off. Listen to them bitch on their way out. Then step out and slam the door behind them. Bathe in the conquest, man.

Watch the inmates run to lunch. Grab the clipboard with the count sheets. Go up the cage. Know that they get counted as soon as they come back. It's a long lunch. Know that most inmates eat in the dining hall on hamburger days. It's a rare meal. Because it's good.

Count them up. They're back. Check off each cell. One, two, check them off. Keep moving. Go fast. Cell 501: one, two. They're still mean-mugging you. Mean-mug them back. Cell 502: one, two. They're standing, looking tired. Cell 503: one. There's still just one, he's pissing again, holding his dick again. Hoping, no doubt, for a female guard to see. You'll fix him to-morrow, the predator. He'll see who's bigger when his mattress disappears. Walk on by. Cell 504: one, two. Their backs are turned. Keep moving. Check off cells.

Give the count to the sergeant. Play cards with the guards in the station. Talk shit during the game. Table-whack, card-slap, and cheat until second shift kicks the door.

It's time to go. Walk out without saying anything. Hear them say, "Fucking first shift." Head to the gate. Line up at the time clock and finger-print scan, single file, no pushing. Pushing slows down the process. The scan can be tricky.

Flow out the gate. Hold it for the guy behind you. Don't let it close. That's serious. That could start a fight. Everyone's ready to leave. Walk into the locker room past the tighty whities and hairy ass crack. Open your locker and gear down. Unstrap.

Shut it nice and slow because you're done slamming. Look at your phone. You have a text from the wife: "Need whole milk & size 3 diapers." Get in your car and go ahead and drive. There are no more gates, just a short winding road through a wide-open field to get you off the property. Watch the jail in the rearview mirror getting smaller. Turn left and drive the speed limit. You can't smell anything. Grab a tissue and blow your nose. The crust is black, but it's out.

And home is where your wife says, "You're on duty" while walking out the door, and your son doesn't do the funny scoot in his pajamas on the hardwood floors anymore. He can walk. And when he's naked and spotless from his bath, not even wearing a freckle yet, he yells, "Run freeeee!" while sprinting around the house, taking corners blind and at full speed, looking for somebody, anybody, to show his little booty-shaking dance to. You catch him because you know that he's going to take a header down the stairs or dive into the dirty laundry, but mostly you catch him because you have about forty-five seconds to diaper him before he pees on the floor. Some-thing he's proud of. The punk.

Gravity

WHAT drew four women wearing matching cat T-shirts to Rockview was a handsome man who murdered three. The oldest said, "We're here to visit Ricky." They stood inside the locker room with smiles. I stood outside with a revolver on my belt, a shotgun in the truck behind me, and a response: Please follow the signs to the visiting room. You're not even close.

What drew a family right next to the main block was their son's bad directions to Penn State. I chased them down, blaring the truck's horn. Their car loaded with pillows and laundry baskets. The mother asked, "Is this East Halls, the freshman dorms?"

I asked back, Seriously?

What drew a grandmother to the flowers around the Rockview sign was a flat tire. But I didn't know it was a grandmother with a flat until I pressed on the gas, sped down the hill, and jammed the brakes behind a silver sedan.

An elderly lady stepped out and waved. She pointed to the tire. A boy in the backseat looked up at the jail.

I radioed Control to say that it was a flat and I was going to change it.

Control said, "Stay in the truck. We can only offer to make a phone call."

I said that it would take ten minutes, tops.

"Stay in the truck," Control said again. "Ask if she needs a tow."

I said I could do it in five minutes.

"Stay. In. The. Truck. Tow?"

So I stayed in the truck, deflated, and put the window down to ask her. She said that she could call her son.

Control told me to tell her, "Remain in your vehicle while you wait." So I did.

Then, "Perimeter," Control said. "Resume your patrol."

So I resumed circling, which I was used to.

When I drove past the grandmother's car, she had her hands up in the international sign for "I don't know."

I was on the edge of purpose there, about to finally help somebody. But had to pull back, as always, and assume the institutional front.

~

I LIVED in Rockview's outer orbit for twenty-seven years before not helping that lady. I drove past the jail for track meets, for karate tournaments, for anything that took me east of town. I never considered stopping. But what finally brought me inside was uniforms. Uniforms for money. I had developed a dependence on them. Rockview's gray and black and made-by-inmate-labor uniform became my fifth.

When I finished with the camouflaged army uniform, I went to college. No more uniforms for me after school—that was my plan. I figured a shirt and tie would be nice for a change. Maybe a sweater in winter. But as it turned out, I wasn't the engineer I thought I was. Two different calculus-teaching grad students named Vladimir told me to drop their classes.

So I found a blue uniform at a water-bottling factory. I drove past Rockview's lights and signs to get there. The factory uniform came with a name patch and a hairnet. I wore both well. But when the factory moved me onto the overnight weekend shift, then the TV factory turned me down, I went to the job center and told the VA guy that I needed a new uniform.

He said that veterans get preference for cop and prison jobs—ten points added to the civil service test. "Takes two years to be a cop," he said. "Four months to be a guard. Pays the same."

I could do that: rules, regulations, hair off the collar, shifts, overtime. Jail was a time-clocked relief. Something concrete, not the derivatives and functions I paid the Vladimirs to fail me at. State jobs let you retire at fifty. The VA guy had me thinking career. Bad guys will always need hired guns circling them. I liked that idea. I even got to wear a tie. A clip-on, sure, but that way I couldn't be choked. And it didn't matter if the pants were wrong—the crotch down low by my knees—they didn't keep me from chasing around cat ladies or wearing a pistol. Those made-by-inmate pants got me fed.

~

WHAT drew the jail to Happy Valley in 1911 was seven thousand cheap acres of forest and farmland. One of the farms purchased was called Rockview. Spring Creek runs through the property. A nearby town stocks the creek with trout.

One inmate and one guard moved in first. Both men lived in a farmhouse known as the Merit House. The idea for the jail, then called the Honor Farm: bring in low-risk inmates and create a self-sufficient and rehabilitative farming community.

But Pennsylvania needed a central location for executions in 1915, so the fence and death house went up, soon followed by the dining hall, gym, and bunker-style main blocks. Most of the original guards came from the nearby White Rock Quarry. In high school, my friends and I hung out in that abandoned quarry. There is a cave halfway down the cliff face. It's cold, wet, full of mud, and it broke a guy's back two or three years after we slid around in it without ropes or helmets or common sense.

Rockview had its own quarry. A bucket line for stones, sand, and mortar ran from the Merit House up the hill. Inmates did some of the labor, but there weren't enough at the beginning, so contractors did most of the work. When the inmate population outgrew the house, they moved into the dining hall. Those men wore civilian clothes and lived nothing like the men confined on the grounds today. They slaughtered their own cows and maintained an orchard. They stayed busy.

But when I drove the truck, I saw an overgrown orchard, fallow fields, and retired cows. Rarely an inmate outside the fence. Most jobs were in the dining hall, the service industry, like the rest of the country. The inmate workweek was thirty hours, just enough to earn money for cable and some peanut butter from the commissary.

The manufacturing jobs at Rockview shut down right after I started. The cannery, leather shop, and upholstery shop closed up, the inmates laid off. I knew about that. I lived on unemployment every winter when the bottling factory turned off the water for six weeks. But plenty of jobs had been manufactured at Rockview—the block worker jobs (jail speak for janitor jobs) filled in for actual trades. Each block had about forty workers banging trash cans down stairs, push-brooming ranges, and just barely raising pulses.

But squeegeeing the showers twice a day at least got a guy out of his cell, made him money, and made him useful for thirty minutes. Rising inmate populations made for more idle inmates. But rising inmate populations also made for rising corrections-officer populations, for which I was thankful. Industry after industry shut down in Happy Valley. White Rock Quarry: open to trespassers only. The TV factory: sold for scrap. The electronics factory where I sorted capacitors for months: vacated. But Rockview, the survivor, kept on incarcerating.

~

WHAT made the patrol truck smell like peanut butter for a week one July was the peanut butter loaded into the shotgun's chamber. Nobody knew who did it.

Every four hours the guards rotated out. We traded the guns and goods. "You good?"

"Yep. Good. You good?"

"Yep. Good."

Then the truck rolled on, at idle speed, by double fences, anti-climb wire, motion sensors, cameras, thirty-foot towers, and cats, groundhogs, and skunks that ate scraps the tower officers threw down. On one side of the fences: green fields. On the other: gray concrete.

If idling counterclockwise, the truck idles past Tower 1, which overlooks the main gate, parking lot, and guard locker room. The truck idles past the fenced-in wood and paint shops and former cannery. Those shops all have different roofs, some square, some stepped, some peaked. After turning left at the corner by Tower 2, the truck idles past the bucket (jail speak for the restricted housing unit, or solitary confinement), a newer stone building. Then past the laundry house, an older stone building. Then past Tower 3, which stands over the fence from the big yard with its two softball fields and weightlifting pavilion. The truck idles past where the jail used to end, at an old fence where Tower 4 sits empty during daylight. The truck idles a little farther, turns left, idles past the maintenance shops opposite the jail. That's a good place to take a leak—not inside, around back. The truck rolls past Tower 5, which stares at the smaller yard with the handball and basketball courts. Turns left. Idles past the largest and oldest block, where one thousand inmates live in two five-story wings. It has a gray concrete finish with ridges and ledges that would be climbable if it weren't for the razor wire. The building is close to eighty feet tall, longer than a football field, and has a central rotunda where the superintendent works on the top floor. The truck idles past the treatment building, with the control center, infirmary, and visiting room with its outside area, its few tables, its fewer umbrellas that don't obstruct the cameras' views. The truck turns left and idles back north to the main gate to idle and turn and idle and turn past the same century-old buildings where thousands of guards have idled away their years until finding a higher-paying uniform or receiving a beating from an inmate or succumbing to heart disease or corruption or just acknowledging that the double-fenced perimeter wasn't worth the money and forced them to seek a paycheck elsewhere. Some retired.

The truck stops only to refuel, to reload guards, to change direction if the guard wants to fight the monotony. I switched once an hour. It didn't help.

In jail, you are what you beat. That beat was called perimeter patrol. That job was out there on the threshold between free and not, green and not, poor and not, and right on the limit of boredom.

~

THE biggest supermarket chain in Pennsylvania has ninety-two stores. I stocked shelves at one in high school. I made the toilet paper displays look like giant rolls of toilet paper. Pennsylvania also has 101 jails when you add up all the levels: county, state, and federal. The state-level jails alone stock fifty thousand inmates a year to be watched, restrained, taught, counseled, medically treated, fed, and circled at idle speed with loaded guns at all times. But the public, the other 12 million Pennsylvanians who aren't doing time, don't know a thing about them unless they're on parole, or visiting Ricky, or breaking down in front of one only to be told to remain in their vehicle by a guard who smells like peanut butter.

After I left, Rockview's administration shut down four of the five towers to save money. In response to the public's concern, the assistant superintendent told a local reporter, "I don't think the public understands what we have here because obviously no one comes here. We don't allow the public to drive by and see exactly what we have."

The public, for sure, doesn't know. Jails are everywhere but nowhere. All the public sees of Rockview is a bunker surrounded by flowers, shrubs, fields, and the ancient ground-down Appalachian Mountains.

As a civilian you can look. Go ahead. But don't stop.

And please leave.

The guard handbook warns, "Employes are prohibited from imparting information to ANYONE not attached to the Institution."

And I never did.

Until I was not an employee anymore. My wife took a job that let me escape. We moved to rural Missouri and I stayed home with our son. Baby number two, our daughter, was on the way. One day I was in charge of two thousand convicted felons. The next, in charge of making grilled cheese. One of my wife's colleagues asked, "What are you, a teacher or what?"

Nothing, was my answer. Which was a first. I had always been a something.

After a year I went back to school and took a writing class. The first essay was going to be about jail. But what came out was everything. So I kept writing—for ten years. It pulled me right back in. And I decided that the reason blue-collar workers don't usually write books isn't because they're dumb or untalented—they're just too damn tired. Energy is energy. It's burned up circling a jail or writing chapters, and there's a finite daily supply.

~

WHAT brought a picketer to Rockview was an upcoming execution. Her sign read, *Stop The Massacre*. I told her she could stand across the street. She told me, "I forgive you." Then I circled for two hours, holding tight to the perimeter until my relief stepped from the control center. He was an oldhead (jail speak for old) guard. I gave him the guns and the goods: You good, oldhead?

"Good, young buck, real good. I hit the street in two months" (jail speak for he was going to retire).

At the time, that was my future speaking. It looked heavy.

He idled away.

I walked through the reinforced double doors, under the wire, between the motion sensors, and through the metal detector. The control sergeant asked me if the grandmother was hot ("Well, was she?") then gave me my next assignment. "D block," he said. "One of their guys went home sick."

I walked through three more doors, then a gate, and saw a middle-aged inmate throw an empty milk carton on the sidewalk. I made him pick it up. He said, "You trippin', CO."

A young inmate sprinted past us. I stopped him and asked why he was running. "Gotta get that money." Which sounded about right. He had a commissary pass. Inmates called all commissary items money.

I kicked on D block's door. The block sergeant told me, "Showers, close 'em up." So I assumed my position at the entrance to the showers. The shower room was 250 square feet of showerheads and soapy men. The steam wrinkled my uniform. The soap stung my nose. I called out, Ten minutes!

And Melvin, that notorious inmate, tiny in size, massive in character, called back, "Fuck yo ten minutes!" I hadn't even noticed him in there.

A soapy man said, "Fucking Melvin."

Another said, "Evil dwarf."

An inmate by the door had a boot print tattoo on his back. And while I considered its meaning, I turned off the water and dared Melvin to turn it back on.

Melvin

ONE afternoon, years after leaving the jail, I watched my daughter play the video game Minecraft. It's like digital Legos with people and zombies and animals. You can build the pyramids of Giza or the Eiffel Tower or a floating pink house made of wool. You can build anything. So what does she build? A jail, of course. And she says to me all sweet-like, "I'm going to do something very bad. I'm going to put babies in the jail." Because you can do that too.

~

THIRD week postacademy I walked with an older guard. He said, "Today's mission: get in, get out, get paid." He used to be a landscaper. Did it until he hurt his back. He told me, "I can make a yard look good. The right length to cut grass is three and a quarter inches. Why not three? Why not four? Because grass don't follow standard measurements. Grass follows grass."

Four inmates in yellow jumpsuits walked out of the control center. Another guard escorted them. Yellow jumpsuits meant they were transfers. Standard uniforms were brown.

One of them, a minisized transfer, was four foot six at most. His jumpsuit was rolled up at the wrists and ankles.

"What," the guard walking with me said. "The fuck is that? Is this juvie now? Day care? Babies 'R' Us?" He yelled to the small man, "Hey, babyGap, don't I know you?!"

The tiny man, acting uninterested, looked at him and yelled back, "I fuck your mother?"

That ex-landscaper with something like ten years in jail stopped walking. I stopped too. Jail had me confused. It was full of violent stories like "That guy threw a dude off the top range last year over a bag of pork rinds," and "That guy decapitated his victim," and "That guy was a chiropractor who raped women coming in for job interviews." Guards told me this while we walked around watching guys sleep all day. They didn't look violent. Just tired. A double murderer told me politely on my second day, "Hey, CO, I'm the night-shift cook. Do you mind turning your radio down? I need my Zs. Otherwise chow will suck . . . more than usual." Then he laughed. Me too. He seemed reasonable. But another guy mean-mugged me for walking in front of him at the mailbox. In his hand: a letter addressed to *Mamma*.

And here was the smallest inmate I had seen openly challenging somebody who had been wearing that uniform for over a decade.

The landscaper ran up to the small man and demanded his ID card, which he didn't have—he had been in the jail all of twenty minutes. "Well," Landscaper said. "Give me your name."

"Melvin."

"Melvin what?"

"Melvin nothing."

"Melvin nothing?"

"Yeah, Melvin. My mother gave me Melvin. So I'm Melvin."

The guard escorting the new inmates said, "His last name is Pang."

Melvin said, "My hurters are called Pang."

"What?" Landscaper asked.

"My hurters."

"Your hurters?"

"My foster parents."

Landscaper paused a long pause. Adjusted his hat. Then said, "Come see me some time, Pang, I work in the AC. You know what that is?"

Melvin said, "That's not my name."

"Administrative Custody, that's the place they send dickheads."

Landscaper veered off to the AC, the place for dickheads, and I kept walking to D block, my assignment for the shift. Melvin wore state-issue brown boots and a straight back. He walked with his chin unnaturally high.

~

UP to that point, I'd been only focused on myself. I mainly wanted to not screw up. I gripped keys tightly. I ironed my uniform. I left the house a half hour early. Here's what I cared about: that deadly force could be used to prevent serious bodily harm to oneself or others, that inmates had to stand for count, that pat-downs included a thorough search of armpits. Never mind that I only found warmth and moisture in those pits. There could be a bulge. Something dangerous. Maybe a ketchup bottle melted into a knife grip around a sharpened nail. That was something to care about.

But then Melvin walked in with his hurter speak.

~

WHEN I got to D block I told the sergeant that I had just met an odd inmate. He said, "Jail odd or free-world odd?"

I said, Both?

He said, "Nope. There is no odd inside."

Jail has its own measurements.

Then he said, "Apparently there's a pile of shit, actual human feces, somewhere up on level 2. Find a block worker to clean it up. Tell me if it contains contraband."

~

AFTER shift I looked Melvin up. He was state-issue, supposed to be living in a youth group home until the age of twenty-one for burglary. But he walked away one night and broke into a house, burned it down with a piece of paper, then tried to enter a second house with a sledgehammer, then stole a gun from a truck outside a third, then went to a fourth and shot himself in the right foot while standing on the porch.

~

ON his second day at Rockview, I saw him in his temporary holding cell. I asked him why he was using his underwear for a do-rag.

"They stunted me. They beat me. They starved me. They got paid to do it." That was his answer.

A sledgehammer, a fire, a gun, and many broken things—that was Melvin's perfect life of demolition. His mother was addicted to crack and other drugs that she used heavily while pregnant with him. The state took him in. But he was abused in foster care. So off to the residential treatment facilities he went. These are the state-funded facilities with missions to help and heal.

But when the helping and healing fails, they pretty much just chemically manage kids until they're old enough for jail. I would work in one later in life as a junior high teacher. Melvin sent me. In essence. He made me want to help.

I would go on to have dynamic classroom conversations with a twelve-year-old who witnessed his father cut his mother's throat (she survived).

Example conversation:

Me, Let's talk math now.

Him, "Let's talk fuck-you-bitch now."

But five minutes later he said, "I'm sorry, Mr. B." Then he hugged me. Which was progress. The first twenty times he had rolled his worksheet into a paper bong.

He also shrieked any time a classmate touched his sweatshirt.

So they all touched his sweatshirt.

Of course.

Another kid left my classroom in handcuffs. He had punched a teacher down the hall in the face because he did not know why.

Melvin's crime spree, the randomness of it, a kid walking around in the night angry, didn't seem so odd. If you were ever to learn that people got paid to hurt you, expect to be confused and angry.

One news article calls him a "mentally challenged man" with an IQ of fifty-eight, which is below the threshold a person can be considered competent to stand trial. Below seventy is classified as feeble-mindedness. His counselor at the residential said he had the mentality of a five-year-old.

As I write this, my daughter is five. She sings. She makes up words. She would be happy to not take a bath for a month.

Melvin committed crimes. And, according to the courts, knew the difference between right and wrong. This is what he was: old enough and dangerous enough for jail. Melvin told the judge, "I'm sorry for what I done."

~

ON his third day at Rockview, Melvin walked onto D block wearing state-issue browns and holding all his possessions in the world: a brown bag of state-issue toiletries. Once he met his celly, an oldhead, and climbed up into his top bunk, I asked Melvin why he was here.

He said, "Too strong to be poor." He rolled over and faced the wall.

I walked down the range. The guy next door was squeezing a pimple on his nose. While I was new in the jail uniform, if inmates spoke to me, they said things like, "How 'bout them burgers?" Small talk. But Melvin spoke about strength and pain and anger.

I heard him tell his celly, "No jail big enough for me."

At the end of the range lay another pile of feces. I backtracked and found a block worker to clean it up. He said, "I'll catch another case if I find the motherfucker doing this." He meant he'd get another criminal case.

I didn't want to catch the motherfucker either.

At Melvin's trial he said that he had made a "bad mistake." He said, "I need help, like serious help." And he got it: eighteen to thirty-six months in a state prison with seven impossible-for-him-to-stay-right years of probation afterward. Which is to say he didn't get any. Which is to say nothing new for him. Which is to say welcome home. Ignore the shit stains.

How to Stop Being Too Poor to Propose

TO work in jail you have to pass the interview. Which means entering a dark room and siting at a table across from five uniformed officers. Spotlights illuminate each officer. Another lone light shines on a pad of paper and pen at your seat. Now answer:

Are you afraid of contracting tuberculosis?
Are you afraid of contracting the AIDS virus?
Are you afraid of contracting hepatitis C? Hepatitis B? Hepatitis A?
Are you afraid of being assaulted?
Are you afraid of being sued?
Are you afraid of the debilitating stress associated with this job?
Are you afraid to work here?
So what are your hobbies?

For the last question, I told them that I loved woodworking, martial arts, and canoeing. I raced my canoe, I told them, down rapids. My girlfriend and I placed fifth in a race the month before. But, I told them, we were just going for survival. No flipping, no lost paddles, no being crushed between our seventeen-footer and the boulders in front of the drunks camped out at the roughest part of the creek.

No laughs or smiles from the officers. Before the interview I had expected my answers to sound like this: I feel my best quality is attention to detail. And: I have no problem staying late or working weekends. Instead, I found myself answering to fear. I hadn't considered fear. I hadn't considered incurable diseases, punches to faces, or public records of litigation and condemnation. It was a pay raise. So to fear I answered: No, I'm sure that the jail has procedures to follow, I'm good with procedures, I'll follow the procedures . . . just what are the procedures? Do we get gloves?

The answer to my question was that when a guard gets a cup of shit liquefied with piss and spit and maybe blood in the face, he has to go to the hospital to pick up a seven-day regimen of pills, which will hopefully kill any life-threatening viruses that may have just swum through the mucous membrane of his eyes and begun the rampant replication, which would only stop once his body was embalmed and wearing its best suit, or sometimes a brand-new suit because maybe his body-that-used-to-be-a-person didn't own a suit yet because it was too young and oblivious to need one, which is why it allowed itself to get the shit cocktail thrown like a fucking mythical rising fastball into its open-but-not-seeing eyes in the first place. But yes you get gloves.

That's not what the major said. But that's what I got from her tone. She mentioned the pill regimen and asked, "Sound good to you?"

I said, Yes, well, no, not good . . . but something like that.

Another officer asked her, "Who's next?" That meant it was time for me to go. I stood, looked at the unmarked pad of paper and said, Thanks.

Two weeks later a letter came and told me that I didn't get the job. So I kept the overnight weekend shift at the water-bottling factory and the reality of my life: that I worked the overnight weekend shift in a water-bottling factory.

~

WHEN those five officers around the table rejected me, the fear message was lost—I only felt the money. What is hepatitis A, really, but a few weeks of fatigue and clay-colored feces? The state will pay you 80 percent of your wages until you're healed up. Enjoy the three months off. More if you can prove your liver's still inflamed.

I stood spinning a bottle labeler for a year thinking about how I should have answered those questions.

~

THEN, after being promoted to water-bottling team leader over a single mother of two and watching her cry because of it—she felt that loss of money hard, that blue-collar pain—a letter from Rockview showed up asking me to come in for another interview.

This time three officers sat in folding chairs in HR and asked me questions like, "Do you hunt?"

I told them that my friend hunted everything. He ate sparrows (he really did). They laughed, and I, at the age of twenty-seven, the college dropout, the failer of first interviews, the bottle-labeling expert, got to learn the ways of correcting men. When the letter came offering me the job, I was happy to sign up for the union. Inmates weren't even a consideration then.

And fear? Please. They had pills for that.

~

SOON after, I took my girlfriend out to dinner. She was a petite and driven graduate student studying French at Penn State. She told good stories. Definitely American dreamy. And while eating ice cream I told her that I loved her more than waffle cones and handed her a ring I'd bought with my MasterCard. And she let me put it on her. We went to sleep that night with the synchronized deep breath that lovers do: long inhale, long exhale.

Then I left the next week to attend the Pennsylvania Department of Corrections Training Academy to learn how to harden myself emotionally, peer into men's anuses, and avoid cups of piss and shit like my life depended on it.

Because it did.

D-Ranging

IN jail, everything bolts to something. Bunks: bolted to the floor. Cabinets: bolted to the floor. Block TVs: bolted to the wall.

On the top level of D block, range 5, inmate Normal, a young guy, reached through his cell bars and gave his rug an underhand toss. It went across the range, through the cage bars, down fifty feet, and landed on top of a card table. That's how inmates reserved tables: first rug won.

"Boom!" he said. "Mine."

The tables: stainless steel, polished, and bolted to the floor in the twenty feet of open space between the cells and outer walls. The cells: enclosed by a hundred-year-old cage. It was hard not to imagine it as a birdcage for something prehistoric and huge and shrieking.

The block sergeant, who weighed 350 pounds and who everyone called Shrek, rang the bell from the bubble (jail speak for glass-enclosed officer station). The doors, all 250 of them, opened.

Inmates bolted down.

Block out! Yard out! Shrek yelled into the PA system.

Normal ran by me and said, "Carpet bomb, CO. You like?" He disappeared into the mass of inmates wearing brown pants and white T-shirts.

The bell meant count was clear, evening yard was open, school was on, chapel too, for almost three hours, until lockdown for the night, final count, and the end of my six days straight on D block. That's how the shifts worked: six on, two off.

The sun, the steam pipes, the shower room, and the 458 bodies on the block radiated heat. The hanging lights glared. The trash stunk.

When the jail was first built, the windows opened by hand crank. But time and grime had knocked the teeth off the gears and bent the shafts and sealed in every degree and breath and slam.

As soon as the inmates cleared the range, I shut cell doors. I went fast. The regular guard in the cage made it a competition. "Last one down," he said, "sits by Shrek tonight."

In three hours we'd be playing spades or hearts in the guard station drinking iced tea and fake-laughing at Shrek's jokes to finish the shift. His iced tea was syrup—that's how much sugar he used. And all his jokes had blowjob punch lines.

Earlier he asked, "Why did God invent women?"

I gave up.

"Blowjobs," he said.

I dreaded it. The jokes. The tea. The cards. He cheated. I had had enough stimulation for one week.

Inmate Normal, the carpet bomber, ran back to his cell before I could shut it. He said, "Damn, CO. Forgot my cup. We playing for shots" (jail speak for a tablespoon of instant coffee).

He had had a busy week too. Lost two cellies to solitary confinement.

After the second, Shrek said, "That means Normal ain't putting out."

Must be, I said.

He said, "I'm talking about blowjobs, Langston."

I got it, I told him.

I never knew what to say to Shrek.

Normal had stacks of soap in his cell. "Air fresheners," he said. "New guy be dying or something." A young guy sat watching Normal's TV. He did smell a bit like death.

I checked on Melvin. Only his celly was there.

He said, "Nothing but a baby, that one. I have to tell him to brush his teeth. Why they put babies in jail?"

Shrek yelled into the PA system, "You, standing on the table! Yes, you. Come here."

From below, I heard Melvin yell back, "But I won!"

He looked tiny down there. He looked like Melvin. His pants around his thighs. His white boxers billowed and bunched up above them. His fists full of lollipops and Hershey bars. The men around him laughing.

Normal played for shots.

Melvin played for candy.

Shrek got serious in the PA, "Come here, young man."

I slammed cell doors, which seemed the right way to do it. The block was loud. The noise had built all day. I first walked into the concrete bunker to the quiet of an extended after-lunch count, not even a toilet flushing. But it was hot, eighty degrees, easily. And when count cleared, most inmates went to yard (always called just "yard" in jail speak, never "the yard") and let me walk the ranges alone in peace. I was damp. My hat itched. I made the rounds. Doors opened. I closed them. I didn't listen to the block announcements. My job was to shut cage doors. So that's what I became. The caged doorman. The bell rang and a few hundred guys came back from yard and ran up and down the stairs and to and from the showers. I saw agitation. It was ninety degrees by then. They crowded me on the ranges. They yelled about the NBA finals going on that night. I walked the rectangular cage. Technically, it was a rectangular prism. It refracted smoky light. A prison prism that I rounded and climbed and sprayed with sweat.

Lines went out. There was the chapel line, the shot line, the right-before-the-evening-meal line when the inmates filed back in line. I left the cage once, for the chili con carne in the staff dining hall. Inmates left for their own chili ration and took their hopeful basketball game expectations with them down the steps. "Pistons by fifteen." I shut doors. "Spurs by ten." I shut doors. "Chili on a hot-ass day like today?" From the cage I watched the last one leave. I shut doors. They came back louder. "Pistons by twenty-moth-erfucking-two!" I shut doors. Shrek called count time, and that's when the screaming started. "Yes! Yes! There will be ball! Yes! Yes! Ball for all!"

Count cleared. Shrek opened the cells and the entire block hit the showers and ran the ranges and ran their mouths and ran out to the yard to buy ice cream and ran down to sit at the benches to watch the TV behind the Plexiglas or to see if Melvin would continue his win streak. He looked happy. He had attention. But when a guard walked close by he quieted down. I slammed doors. My hands were sore. Then there was the game's opening jump ball and the block became a great sweating bellowing furnace that slammed me back.

Scraps of yellow paper covered the ground like confetti. Used in-mate passes. Library: get a pass. Doctor's appointment: get a pass. Coun-selor, visiting room, gym, chapel, and psychiatrist: get passes, make sure they're signed. This, from what I saw, writing passes, was Shrek's primary occupation.

I caught Normal on the wrong range. I told him that since it was the first time I caught him—and didn't know what do about it anyway—I'd give him a free pass. I told him, Stay on your range, please?

"Ten–four, CO. My bad."

He held up his scratched-plastic coffee cup. "This is shot fourteen. I'm buzzing, CO. Buzzing!" Fourteen cups of coffee sounded lethal. "I know a guy who snorts it," Normal said. "I'm doing twenty today. Twenty god-damn shots!"

It seemed too loud on the block that night. Too chaotic. Deranged. I saw a guy upside down, legs hanging outside the cage, body inside, doing sit-ups. I made him get down. I saw another standing on top of a trash can and wearing a folded-newspaper hat. I told him to take it in (jail speak for go to your cell). My first five days weren't like that. Inmates slept. But the heat and noise kept on coming. The game made the third quarter. The fire alarm went off every fifteen minutes with a droning Whoooop Whoooop Whoooop that was so loud that if somebody had driven by on the street, and if the windows were open, that somebody would have believed a riot was in progress. The heat set it off.

Shrek yelled, "Melvin, young man, I'm not telling you again!" Inmates and staff were learning Melvin's name.

I watched the sun lower through the brown windows from range 5. The volume stayed high. Inmates and guards milled around by the TV and phones: inmates in brown and white, guards in gray and black, all of us watching the clock. I willed Shrek to ring the bell.

And he did.

I ran down the steps against the flow of inmates. I was going for the count sheets. And even though we had no space, and even though everyone was sprinting, nobody knocked shoulders with me.

Then something broke above me. It sounded how a car accident sounds: big bangs with glass rain. Inmates screeched. I looked up so see that three windows on range 5 were broken. I paused, expecting to see an escape rope hanging out. But saw the bars still intact. Somebody yelled, "Can't take the goddamn heat!"

When I made the bubble, I told Shrek what had happened.

He said, "No shit? I'm going to make them pay." He sent me back up on a hopeless mission to find the guys who broke them. But before I left he asked me, "Want to know the secret to straight-up happiness?"

Sure.

"A blowjob."

The doors banged shut on the ranges. Inmates locked themselves in. Something they didn't usually do. I guessed that the guilty were nowhere near range 5 anymore—guilty for the windows, I mean—but I made it look good for Shrek and took the steps two at a time.

Up top I saw nothing except the state-issued soap used to break the glass sitting on the frames of the former windows—the bars and screens kept them out of the parking lot. Fifty feet below, little cubes of safety glass were all over the floor. Everyone was in his cell. The ranges were clear. But still banging. That was a good time in jail. For the inmates. I felt them watching me. Normal asked me through the bars, "Find anything, CO? Who did it, CO? Want some help, CO?"

I radioed Shrek, *Range 5 is clear. They used bars of soap.*

"Ten–four," he radioed back.

The sun set. There was no sense rushing down. I had the count sheets. I had investigated the jail crime to the full extent of my ability. The window-breakers did me a favor anyway. Wind blew through the bars. It smelled like the Pennsylvania I used to know. It was cool and full of night. It cured the fire alarm. It smelled free and fresh and a few glass cubes fell from the frames and flashed like sparks on the way down.

In one hour I knew I'd be driving home with the windows down to try and blow the public-restroom stink off my uniform. I would take the long way, the route through the farms with their tractor-cracked roads, streaking lightning bugs, and sleeping cows. Home meant AC, even if it was only a window unit. That was straight-up luxurious. My fiancée was even there, probably grading her students' papers and listening to classical music at the table I had just bolted together. The talk the night before: we should try for kids right away. How different it was eight miles away.

But then Shrek made threats over the loudspeaker about how he was going to keep the lights on and keep guards running the ranges until somebody owned up for the windows. He said that he was going to get maintenance to come and turn the heat on. "Bet me," he echoed. "Bet me." He was faking it but had to say something—it was his block.

He delayed count fifteen minutes to be dramatic, but after the phone rang—no doubt the control center asking him for numbers—he rang the bell for at least a minute straight, until the hammer had to be red hot, and called, "Count time! Count time! Be standing! Be visible! Lights on! Count time! Count time!"

"Fuck your count!" inmates yelled.

"Fuck your lights!" inmates yelled.

I counted—all 458 inmates. We were short that night. Usually you only counted two ranges. The regular guard followed me. It was loud. The game was getting close, and the broken windows and wind energized the block. The ranges glared. Cell lights were on then, as required. I checked them off. We started at the top. Normal saluted. Melvin giggled.

We finished in ten minutes. My headache dimmed. And for the first time since clocking in, I wasn't sweating.

No more caged rounds for me. No more doors. No more hot breath and smoke and slams.

Down in the bubble I gave Shrek the count: all.

Over the speaker he said, "You can forget about soap tomorrow."

Sunday was soap day. Every inmate got a fresh bar.

Inmates screeched again—a bullshit technical foul was called in the last minute of the game. Shrek thought it was him who had them fired up. "That's right, bitches," he said to the four of us guards.

Then the inmates chanted, "Lights! Lights! Lights!" They wanted them out.

Shrek pumped his fist in rhythm with the cheer. "You break my windows? I'm leaving 'em on!"

"Fuck you! Turn up the heat!" It sounded like Normal. His voice was hoarse.

Shrek laughed and cut the lights.

The game was over.

Up in the cage I saw lights still on in some cells, figures moving, cigarettes streaking, TVs flickering blue. The wind blew through cage. The only noise was the occasional tick of falling glass. An oven cooling off.

Nobody spoke for a long minute. I sat on the counter and I took off my hat.

Shrek leaned back almost horizontal in his desk chair. The bolts creaked. "Seventeen years here," he said. "Seventeen years, and there's only one thing that beats final count . . ."

He looked up at the cage.

He looked at us.

He said, ". . . and that's a blowjob."

And I laughed. I actually did. It was funny. Anything was. Then.

The Man Factory

A MAN becomes the Man in a Pennsylvania state prison after only five weeks at the Pennsylvania Department of Corrections Training Academy. The academy's an old brick children's hospital with cherub statues on the roof and a pepper-spray chamber out back.

I walked under the cherubs with my gym bag. The duty sergeant working the desk, a young guy, about six foot five and 240 pounds of muscle, said, "S'up."

My room came with a camouflage bedspread. The window was painted shut. Other cadets walked from the parking lot carrying duffle bags and rolling suitcases. Old oaks and green grass surrounded the building.

~

THE top Man at the academy, Lieutenant Rice, yelled into his microphone, "Welcome, Class 615!" We sat on folding chairs in the gym. Word was inmates beat him badly in a riot fifteen years earlier. Cadets whispered about razor-wire scars. He said, "The food here is better than anywhere else in the DOC. Period."

Rice introduced the seven sergeants on the stage. There was the redneck, the rugged lady, the one with a bad haircut, the fat one, the gnarly one-eared one, the intimidating one, and the muscly one who signed me in. They stood, arms crossed, and labeled us the same, no doubt. We had the fat cadets, the redneck cadets, the tough-looking cadets, and the one cadet dressed all in black with spikes on his boots. Most of us ex-military. There were only two black guys. The few women, maybe fifteen, were almost all nurses, counselors, or kitchen staff. I put the goatee percentage at 95 percent.

I decided, right then, to grow my own.

Lieutenant Rice told us a cadet had already been asked to leave. He had showed up drunk. "Come talk to me anytime," Rice said. "But chances are, if I have to find you, you're done. Kicked out."

Rice told us to yell, "DOC proud!" So we yelled. Then he said, "Return the chairs to the back of the gym and hit your racks." So we returned the chairs and hit our racks.

~

CLASS 615 was 180 goatees strong, but they split us into three smaller groups. We wouldn't get our uniforms until week five, so it was civvies for everyone: polo shirts and jeans seemed to be the unspoken dress code. I bought two polos after the first day.

The Man assigned to my class was the fat sergeant from the stage, a bald man with one squinty eye. He had three rolls of flesh on the back of his neck. The cadets called him the Vanilla Gorilla.

He said that our classroom was originally the ER, then announced, "This is what we are going to do in the next five weeks: get through this." When he talked, only half of his mouth moved. It looked like he was recovering from a stroke. But he walked fine.

We introduced ourselves by giving our names and favorite movies.

In the class we had a lot of *Rocky*s and *Full Metal Jacket*s. A guy with a flattop said, "I'm a big movie buff. So it's hard to decide . . . but it has to be *Die Hard*. The first one."

"Yes!" another guy with a flattop said.

A guy at my table said that the ladies in high school called him Chocolate Thunder. Vanilla Gorilla loved this. He half-smiled.

I said my movie was *Seven Samurai*. Nobody seemed to recognize it. There was an actual pause.

Seven Samurai is about seven samurai warriors with different skills coming together to save a farming village from bandits. They take the job for rice and honor only. Working for rice, I felt, everyone would at least relate to.

At a podium, Gorilla gave us our first lesson: how to talk to inmates. He read a chapter from what he called *The Book of the Man*—which was a jail-policy book.

He read that when speaking to an escalated inmate (jail speak for an inmate yelling something like "I got nobody left. Nobody. Know what that's like?") you should appeal to him as an equal by repeating phrases like "I understand where you're coming from" and "That must be hard."

Then Gorilla said, "But this is how it really works. Don't say, 'Calm down.' Don't say, 'Relax.' They won't calm down or relax. Any questions?"

A cadet asked, "It's okay to shake an inmate's hand?"

"Well, yes," Gorilla said, which was a surprise. "But that doesn't mean you let any dickheads grit on you" (jail speak for mean-mug you).

~

THEY bused in inmates from a local jail to cook our food. I stared at them in the dining hall.

I was not going to let them grit on me.

An obese inmate who wore an all-white uniform and hairnet pushed a plate with meatballs and a brick of garlic bread at me. I did not say thank you. Just gave him a nod to see what he would do. He nodded back. I sat, back to the wall, watching him.

~

SUBJECTS from "use of force" to "use of restraints" changed hourly. Gorilla read from *The Book of the Man* and taught to the tests while I daydreamed about paydays.

Ultimately, the academy's mission wasn't to turn people into perfect guards. It was to get people used to the idea of being the Man over other men. It's a process. It costs money to hire guards and get them uniformed, and the state wanted to keep them in that uniform for more than a week.

The process was mostly successful. Of the five Rockview cadets, I was the first to leave after three years. But a cadet who graduated six months after me resigned after only one day at Rockview. I heard him say, "Some shit's going to kick off in here," after being surrounded in the crush of inmates headed to breakfast.

Gorilla told us, "Today, you can't just throw a guy in jail with a key and tell him to run the place. But that's how we used to do it."

That first Friday, five days in, he stopped me and said, "Your goatee looks like butt. Shave."

So I shaved.

~

AT home that weekend, my fiancée asked, "What did you learn?"

How to escalate a killer.

"How's that?"

Calm down, honey. Calm down.

She gave a look and went back to writing. She was halfway through her PhD program.

The joke is, I had so much promise. There I was, a veteran working my way through college to be an engineer. My technical drawings were the best in my intro-to-engineering class. I was president of the Penn State Martial Arts Group. A leader. Until she walked into my karate class one night. And that was it. I dropped out of school and retreated to a factory.

But that's just the joke. Really, I was tired of orders. Call it an overload. In the army, walking to the chow hall risked having one of the thirty thousand soldiers who outranked me let me know he outranked me by having me pick up cigarette butts or straighten my beret or tuck in the one inch of exposed bootlace that came loose while picking up cigarette butts. I didn't even smoke. College felt the same. One of my professors told us we couldn't use blue pens, only black. Never-ending authority. If this was life, I might as well get paid for it.

My fiancée just happened to come along at a moment when, if I were more self-aware and resourceful, I should have gone backpacking across Europe instead of dropping out.

I left her alone and read a well-respected book written by a journalist who had worked as a prison guard for a year. He wrote seventy-three pages on the academy.

I wasn't convinced it deserved eight.

~

I TOOK every meal in the dining hall and got used to the obese inmate. We nodded to each other on every exchange. I didn't stare him down anymore.

There was a good weight room at the academy. At night it was empty except for Sergeant Gnarly-One-Ear, who rode the bike or benched. He always came over and talked and held the heavy bag for me. He said that he was taking a lieutenant slot in Pittsburgh and was looking for an apartment. "Hopefully one over a bar." Wearing shorts and a sweatband, he didn't seem so gnarly.

I just wanted to get through the school. The tests were easy. A 70 percent on anything passed. The challenge was the method of it all. Having Redneck Sergeant make me do pushups because of a wrinkle on my bed only to report to class fifteen minutes later for lessons on how to be the Man over killers of men confused me. I was not authorized to make the killers do pushups.

But Gnarly said, "Good and solid" about my punching.

~

THREE weeks in, Rugged-Lady Sergeant led a combat lesson. Two cadets posed as inmates. She said, "Step 1 for breaking up a fight: wait for backup." Gorilla moved behind one fake inmate, she the other. Then she said, "Step 2: break them up." And she pulled the one cadet's head back so hard by his hair that he later complained of whiplash. Gorilla grabbed the other by the arms.

Then we were told to eat. So we ate.

Then we were told to report to the gas chamber. So we reported.

Then we were grouped together by fours and ordered into the gas chamber. So my group stepped in as ordered.

Redneck Sergeant wore a gas mask and pepper-sprayed us. It closed my lungs. I fought panic. Intimidating Sergeant, chiseled, tall, came in to taunt us. He wasn't wearing a mask. He said that he was immune to pepper spray. Then he said, "Why you crying, cadets? You better sound off with 'DOC proud!,' cadets."

Chocolate Thunder was standing next to me. He gagged once. Then puked on my sneakers. Intimidating Sergeant covered his mouth when he saw that. "Pepper spray I can take," He said. "But not puking."

I retched.

I wasn't immune to anything.

We yelled, "DOC proud!" and left the chamber and I washed my sneakers off at the spigot and retched again.

Then we were ordered up to the shooting range to be teargassed. So we walked up to be gassed.

Sergeant Redneck popped a gas grenade and ordered us to walk through the smoke and breathe it.

We walked through holding our breath. We laughed. We defied the Man. We fake coughed to make it look painful.

Then we were told to clean up and have a good night. So we cleaned up and had a good night and I wondered if I was going to ever know what to do with myself once all the ordering stopped.

~

BACK in the gym for the partner baton drills, Gorilla walked the perimeter of the action massaging his eyelid that wouldn't close. He leaned his head back and squeezed in an eye drop. He watched me for a few moves and said, "For a second there, I could have sworn I was watching Wesley Snipes."

So I did it right? I asked.

"Different," he said.

I slowed down after that.

Then Gorilla yelled out, "Lunch!" So we did lunch.

Meal-Line inmate spoke to me. He said, "You should take the bean paste." That was the vegetarian meal of the day.

I looked around before asking, it's good?

"Better than the seafood salad."

I told him that I would take it then, and thanks.

Not that it made us brothers. But I had made contact. Inmates weren't so alien. Inmates even spoke my language: food. The bean paste was good, as bad as it sounds. The sorry bastards around me ate their seafood salad sandwiches while trying to kill the taste with hot sauce.

~

UP on the shooting range we fired revolvers and shotguns. I was all over the target.

The range master, Sergeant Bad Haircut, told me, "When firing the pistol, visualize pushing the bullet toward the target." It was martial arty and my shot group tightened right up. He cut his own hair to save money. He shaved the sides and back but left the top a red mop. I never saw him smile.

Gorilla told us, "This will get you jammed up: being too friendly, or too hard. Just be professional." Haircut kept it professional.

One cadet couldn't hit the target with a shotgun for all the visualization in the world. Haircut worked with him. But it didn't help. Lieutenant Rice had to find that cadet. Kicked out. Another cadet failed the hazardous materials test three times and Rice found him. Another cadet showed up late to class four times and Rice found him. Another found Rice on his own and asked to leave. He said the whole job felt wrong.

~

GORILLA said, "Tell the inmate to pull his foreskin back. Give it a 360-degree visual inspection." Which made me miss the bottle factory. I ran the label machine there. I fed it labels and glue, and it fed me. I could accept that. I prayed for hurricanes—bottled water sales triple during hurricanes—which meant overtime, which meant everything to a guy who charged his computer and a year and a half of college failure on his credit card. I felt communion with the labeler. We were comfortable. We did not inspect foreskins.

But it paid me to be poor.

~

OUR uniforms came in garbage bags. Monday of week five we wore them. The nametag read, "CO1 B. Langston." My label. Meal-Line inmate laughed when he saw me. He said, "You're all official and shit now." Then asked, "Tater tots, CO?"

~

GORILLA showed my class the type of keepers he preferred. Keepers are clips that attach to a guard's belt. You clip your key rings to them. He liked the cheap all-metal kind. His used to be black, but the paint had chipped off and all that was left was grayish metal. "It does the job. Nothing more," he said.

Keeper is also jail speak for guard.

~

ON graduation day, Gorilla said, "Forget everything I said."

I locked in every word.

My class graduated outside under the cherubs, and everyone got a certificate. Then we put away the folding chairs and made room for class 616, which would be coming in less than forty-eight hours. It was Friday. All the sergeants were there, those seven warriors working for Rice and maybe something else that I hadn't learned to identify yet. Rice said, "You did fine work. Now do more." Nothing was special for lunch. Meal-Line inmate told me good luck. I said the same then started that Sunday dressed in my title and uniform for the massive machine labeled the Pennsylvania Department of Corrections.

In a factory you learn by doing. You keep the labeler glue pots an inch low so they don't boil over when a bottle with no cap falls in. In a jail you learn by doing. You inspect foreskins. You don't say calm down. You don't say relax. And you shake, you really do, you shake the first time you walk, all official and shit, through that gate.

Strip, Separate

THIS was life after the academy: Strip searches. Gorilla said, "This is a part of the job. Earlobe to asshole, inspect it all. Do the steps. This is for the good of the institution. So look close. And if you're ashamed to look at another man's penis, this is the time to grow up."

THIS is what I was thinking: will "earlobe to asshole" be on the test?

In the army I went through a combat life saver school. That school was two weeks of watching gory videos and bandaging dummies. For an amputation, we tightened the tourniquet on the rubber dummy's arm until the pretend bright red bleeding stopped. For a sucking chest wound, we taped plastic over the pretend hole on the rubber chest. To diagnose a lower lumbar fracture, we checked for a pretend priapism on the rubber crotch. We combat-saved our dummies over and over until the final exam when we had to partner up and give each other IVs, real human IVs. I got my partner on the first stick. He got me on the third.

That's what I expected for the strip test: a real human experience.

We partnered up for the stripping and took turns playing the inmate, but did it dumbed-down, with our clothes on. We all passed and Gorilla said, "This is how I feel right now: proud. Take an extra twenty for lunch." And I didn't strip a person for real until at Rockview.

THIS is what gets inmates strip-searched: anything. Inmates working outside the jail cutting grass or picking up trash along the highway get stripped at the gate, out and in, no exceptions. Before and after inmates hug and kiss their visitors—no tongues allowed—they're stripped and inspected, every inch. Court hearings, security investigations, lockups, shakedowns, hospital trips, cell searches, and threats on staff all have that one thing in common, too—the inmate gets naked, at least once. Gorilla said, "This is why we do all this: it prevents escape, it prevents contraband, it keeps the jail safe. Mostly."

THIS is who brings in most contraband: staff. Ninety-nine percent of the time, when a staff member breaks a rule, it's to an inmate's benefit. Rockview was locked down for three days when two mobile phones were found in a bathroom vent—all two thousand inmates had their cells and selves searched. The state police discovered that a night-shift guard was paying for the phone service. The jail fired him. Hidden with the phones was a pocket pussy in a dirty sock. And even though there's no actual proof that the guard brought in the pocket pussy, we still called him the pimp: the pink plastic pimp.

THIS makes the stripping job harder: old guards. Not all guards made inmates take everything off. Basically, the longer a guard worked at the jail, the less of a chance he'd make them strip naked. Complacency, it's called. Usually, guards were alone with the inmates, so guards could, if they wanted to, bypass steps. I didn't, so sometimes I got a complainer. When I did, it ruined the flow. I had to stop and explain that yes, I was *really* going to look at his ass, and that no, I didn't actually *enjoy* looking at his ass. Some inmates just complained to complain, which was fine. I know I would. I felt exposed during the strip test, bending over in my pants.

THIS is the worst strip-search scenario for guards: being videotaped. Certain situations, like after fights, require a permanent record of a strip search—to document damage or weapons. The required witnessing lieutenant always says things like "Have fun" and "*Analyze* everything," to be funny. If you laugh, you look like a sadist on the tape. If you don't laugh, you've got an attitude problem, according to the lieutenant. There's no avoiding it, though: if you work at a jail long enough, and you're a man in a man's jail, you'll be videotaped looking at another man's penis.

THIS is where inmates get stripped: cells, bathrooms, the gym, the cages in the bucket, they all worked. But I stripped most guys in the Shack. It sat at the main gate. Inmate-built, the Shack had vinyl siding, a linoleum floor, small windows near the roof, a bench, a heater, and a nail in the wall for the strip-search logbook. The Shack was small, ten feet by five feet maybe, but you could get two guys going at once in there. Do it right and you had one guy naked at all times. There was rhythm to it: one strips, one dresses, you mark the logbook, you call out "next."

THIS is how long it takes to get to the naked truth: nine steps.

THIS is step 1: order the inmate to undress. As he removes his clothes, inspect every article. Gloves on, feel every seam. Empty all pockets. Look for modifications, patches on the inside, openings in the collar, strings for hanging contraband down the legs. Unroll all cuffs.

"Made by Inmate Labor." That's what the tags say on both inmate and guard uniforms. Inmates get brown. Guards get black and gray. All are single-stitched for laughs. The crotches are the problem. They blow out after one year.

During a pat search on a cook leaving the chow hall, my hand hit something heavy and solid below his crotch. I asked what it was. He said, "What do you think it is? My junk." I took him to the bathroom and ordered him to strip. He wouldn't at first. But after five minutes of my promises that I wouldn't write him up if he complied, and my threats that he'd get a trip to the bucket if he didn't, I got him out of his pants. His boxers were cinched tight around his thighs and bulging. It wasn't his junk making them bulge. It was sugar. Six pounds of it in baggies—I weighed it later. He said he needed it for his coffee.

THIS is step 2: order the inmate to hold his hands out in front of him, to spread his fingers, then to flip them over.

Every other inmate had a hand tattoo: a cross, a spider web, a teardrop, a scribbled 88 (a white supremacist thing. H is the eighth letter in the alphabet. So 88 means HH, which means Heil Hitler). A poor man's jailhouse tattoo gun is just a staple and the ink from a BIC pen. Most guys only have tattoos on their left hand. Which makes sense. The majority of jailhouse tattoos are self-inflicted, and about 90 percent of the world is righthanded.

THIS is step 3: order the inmate to open his mouth, to pull out his cheeks, then to lift his tongue. Have him remove his dentures or partials. Look up his nostrils at the same time you check his mouth.

Tardive dyskinesia is a rare side effect of the antischizophrenic drug Thorazine. People with it have involuntary and repetitive body movements, usually in their faces. One of the inmates, who always carried a Bible, had it. Every five minutes his mouth opened as wide as it could go and his tongue muscled out to his chin. His eyes squinted from the strain. He did it while talking, eating, and singing—he sang in the jail choir. I can guarantee that he never tried to smuggle anything in his mouth. But during a search, for appearances, I checked his mouth anyway. Skip it, and the stripping just became personal. Gorilla said, "This is how you treat every inmate: the same."

THIS is step 4: order the inmate to turn his head to each side and bend his ears forward. Look in and behind each. A little piece of anything can be rolled up in toilet paper and pasted in any fold on the body like a spit wad.

A twenty-year-old inmate, in for five DUIs, had tingling sensations in his right ear for two weeks. He woke up one morning in severe pain. He went to the jail doctor. The doctor flushed a bug out of his ear, an earwig. After the flush, that inmate went by "Rat." You know, because he was bugged.

THIS is step 5: order the inmate to run his fingers through his hair. Have him remove any wigs or toupees.

I've only seen one inmate with a toupee. An oldhead, and his hair hat was ten years older than me—I asked.

Another guy had a fist-sized, fleshy growth on the left side of his head. No hair on the lump, like it had been rubbed off. I stripped him after a concert in the gym. All three hundred inmates in attendance got stripped. Another keep-the-jail-safe rule. He wasn't embarrassed about the lump. He called it his mood cyst. It turned red when he was mad.

THIS is step 6: order the inmate to lift his arms, visually inspect his armpits.

Not every inmate could afford deodorant from the jail commissary, so the poor ones—called indigent by the state—used the state-issued bars of soap instead. Crusty and yellow, that's how the soap looked—their pits, too.

Jail jobs for inmates, like single-stitching uniforms, paid nineteen to seventy-nine cents an hour—minus taxes. So after buying the necessities (tobacco, instant coffee, and Honey Buns) from the commissary, inmates had choices to make. They could buy deodorant, or buy the three bags of chips they owe to the card shark in the next cell. That's why some used the soap. Those bars of soap also worked for washing clothes, smashing windows, and putting inside a sock to beat a man unconscious, or, at least, bloody.

THIS is step 7: order the inmate to lift his penis and scrotum, then to separate the two. If uncircumcised, order the inmate to pull his foreskin back.

Mumbles was a sex offender with a speech impediment who lived in the Special Needs Unit. Guard-given nicknames are cruel—always. And Mumbles was orange when I first stripped him. I had to know why. He told me, "Hep C." He was jaundiced. At Christmas, the chapel filled for his solo performance of "Silent Night, Holy Night." It was one of the jail's traditions, and an honest good time.

Another guy named Benders, who lost all his front teeth to meth, got busted for humping Mumbles. But before being sent to the bucket—an automatic ninety days for sex acts—Benders filled his pants with toilet paper and lit them on fire. He said he was ashamed. A month later, when I stripped Benders during a shakedown (jail speak for every cell and asshole searched) in the bucket, I couldn't tell whether or not he had foreskin. That's how bad the scarring was. And for the first time ever, I skipped a step.

THIS is step 8: order the inmate to turn around, to lift his left foot and wiggle his toes. Repeat for the right foot.

Jail socks are cheap, linty. That's why the floor was always dirty in the Shack—sock lint. Once a month inmates got a new pair. They lasted one week. One day if the inmate went for a jog in the yard.

I'm no expert, but ugly seems to be the rule when it comes to men's feet. Or maybe I am an expert. I've been through a lot of step 8s, more than seven hundred.

THIS is step 9: order the inmate to bend over and to spread his buttocks.

What to look for is a string. A string coming from the ass. Strings are for the quick and easy removal of, say, two lighters wrapped in a plastic bag, or a cell phone. The strings are hard to see. They're usually black so they blend in with the hair. The ass hair. It's pretty easy to turn any string black. Shoe polish works.

If you see a string, don't pull it. Never pull the string. Contact a lieutenant. A lieutenant verifies, then contacts medical. Medical does the removing. Make sure it's a string. There's usually some rolled up bits of toilet paper, so you have to be sure. Use a flashlight when in doubt.

The trick to get through step 9 is to only look for what doesn't belong. Look for those strings, or the end of a condom. Don't look at the dingleberries or hemorrhoids—work that tunnel vision.

THIS is what I found stripping: one suspicious-looking hollowed-out pencil. At least a hundred loaves of bread (an entire loaf was down the sleeve of one guy's shirt). A case worth of the yellow plasticware from the chow hall, mostly butter knives. A few hundred pounds of jail meat wrapped in napkins: turkey burgers, chicken legs, Salisbury steaks, seafood salad. A thong converted from boxers. A bread bag full of ice. A dozen razor blades extracted from the BIC razors sold at the commissary. A nine-inch mop-handle whack (jail speak for club). Five and a half dead cockroaches—four were in the pants cuff of one inmate—not contraband, just nasty. Enough trash (toilet-paper wads, ketchup packets, old write-ups, passes, whatever) to fill a dozen full-sized trash bags. And a love note to one of the jail's prostitutes. He sold blowjobs for Snickers bars. Everyone called him Snickers. Even the superintendent. The opening line of the note: *So you have Hep C, what else?*

Contraband includes any modified item or items in excess. I found a bag of forty oranges under a guy's bunk. That was excess. He was going to make hooch (jail speak for jail wine). Extension cords are the most modified item in the jail. Inmates stick paper clips and disassembled nail clippers into the socket end. Anything metal works, the thicker the better. Plug it in and it'll boil water instantly. It's called a stinger. I found eight of them.

THIS is why we confiscate any food taken from the dining hall: food poisoning, jail fauna, sour-milk bombs. Meat spoils—inmates didn't have refrigerators. But they had roaches, field mice, and great aim when it came to throwing a two-week-old carton of curdled milk at the bubbles. The two big blocks (A and D, 450+ inmates each) got bombed the most. The bubbles were in the corner by the door. They had tin roofs and windows for shields, but the sour milk, the gag-able clear liquid part, ran and soaked into the metal seams and windowpanes and layers of paint. After a bomb was the only time those blocks didn't smell like cigarettes and piss.

THIS is how much all the dumb shit is worth: something. The entire jail economy was a barter system. A pound of sugar stolen from the chow hall might get a broke inmate two bags of chips and a bottle of instant coffee.

The de facto jail currency was Kite, a pouch of roll-it-yourself tobacco, which cost about a dollar from the commissary. The pouches were green; inmates even called it money. A jailhouse tattoo gun, made from a Walkman's innards, a guitar string, and tape, cost something like thirty Kite.

Kite was the standard, but inmates hoarded everything. A few guys on each block ended up with forty rolls of toilet paper or three dozen blankets. Once a month, minimum, each block ran out of toilet paper. That was when the TP hoarders made their Kite.

And each block had a couple of inmates who had a little extra of everything. Those guys ran stores from their cells. The markup was 25 percent. They sold three-dollar packs of batteries for four Kite. Businessmen, they called themselves. Or hustlers. A hustler would get an extra hat and trade it away for a bag of chips. Then the hustler who bought the hat would sell it for anything worth more than the chips. It didn't matter how much he made—a ten-cent profit got the hat resold. That kept happening. The hat would be sold from hustler to hustler until it made it around the block and back to the guy who had it stolen from him in the first place. And he'd buy it back with one of the twelve dirty towels he had stolen from the laundry. All this, a hat hustler told me, passes the time.

Some inmates who had nothing ended up working for others. Six soups (jail speak for ramen noodle packs) got you a haircut (five for the barber, one for the lookout), a Honey Bun got your laundry washed, an Oatmeal Cream Pie got your toilet scrubbed, and a Snickers bar, well, you already know what that got you.

THIS is what some guards talked about to avoid the reality of stripping another man: sports. Weather. Parole-board dates. The latest staff member fired for bringing in implements of masturbation. How the jail used to be, you know, in the good old days before insurance copays and when the dining hall still served real steak. Small talk isn't just for parties. Usually it's one-sided. The guard does all the small-talking. Inmates thought it was weird—which it was.

THIS is when Gorilla said it was okay to laugh around an inmate: when it's with him.

Interpersonal communication is supposed to involve sensory channels besides speech. I knew exactly what that meant when I was stuck stripping the guys who just dug a ditch, shovelful by muddy shovelful, down by the cow pasture in August. The Shack at the gate didn't have windows or AC or vents or breathable air after thirty ditch diggers stripped down.

Interpersonal communication stresses the use of eye-to-eye contact, but that's tough, logistically, at step 9. And body language, Gorilla told us to watch that. One inmate flexed every time in a flying Superman pose for armpit checks.

Proper communication was important, though. Especially for telling somebody twice my size, when I was in a confined space alone with him, to take off his pants so I could confiscate his six-pound sugar diaper. And then, when I was holding the warm, sweaty thing, I didn't scowl. And I didn't look down at the absurdity of what I was holding and laugh, unless he laughed. Then it was okay.

THIS is the most unexpected find: soon after the academy there was a jail-wide shakedown and I found myself at Melvin's cell. He said, "You again?"

I said, Me again.

He said, "You love me?"

I saw him often, which made sense. Rockview's fenced-in acreage wasn't so big, and he never left. I would say hi. He would say, "S'up, dummy."

Shakedowns worked like this: strip inmate, cuff inmate, search inmate cell, move on to the next inmate and cell. We did the steps and I cuffed him.

He told me, "You bend. You spread. You see how it feels." I found scribbled-on papers in his cell. An army scene on one: kid-like tanks and kid-like planes shooting each other across the page. On another: a scrawled naked woman with huge tits and spread legs, her face dominated by two large nostrils. No mail from anyone. No contraband either, just candy wrappers and torn-up sheets. I threw the sheets in the trash. It looked like he was braiding bracelets. I stepped out. Typically, inmates turned their wrists to make it easier for you to get the cuffs off. I appreciated that. But when Melvin did it, turned his child-like wrists just so, I felt myself grimace. It was an involuntary thing.

I got the cuffs off and looked around and made like my back was hurting from the bend.

He went right to organizing his drawings. He put a jail one on top: bars, a bed, a toilet. Written at the top: *My Crib.*

THIS is who bends: most everyone, eventually. Inmates, guards, even the pigeons that lived on top of the dining hall adapt. Those pigeons never left: born, bred, then dead inside the fence. They got fed year-round by inmates who threw them bread and biscuits and chicken legs from the dining hall. And those pigeons stripped the chicken to bones. I didn't judge them for eating their cousins.

Some inmates rushed through the whole stripping process on their own in four seconds. They did it with their arms flapping, mouth gaping, tongue dangling, toes wiggling, then ended it with a quick turn for an ass-spreading bow. After displays like that, all I could ever tell was whether or not they had rhythm. So I made them do it again. Which I used to think was cruel and unusual punishment—for me—and used to make me question my purpose in life.

When I stripped my first inmate a week after graduating the academy, I barely looked, didn't breathe, and wanted a shower when it was over. My first real human experience stripping made me skip lunch. But after two hundred guys, the search didn't disgust me anymore. I could probably have eaten a tuna salad sandwich while doing it. It's easy to strip another man after you find a five-inch wooden shank in his pocket and hear his casual excuse: "I forgot it was in there."

The entire process can be done thoroughly and professionally in one minute. Time enough to grow up.

I even had a strip-search dream. It wasn't so disturbing, just a work dream, the same as handing out toilet paper or socks.

Everyone was working in jail. Inmates cooked, mopped, barbered, hustled—some even talked their way into getting cell phones. Other inmates worked to keep their prejail life alive. Jewelry was contraband, except wedding rings, so inmates, to keep their piercings open, used the teeth from combs. I saw those black spikes in ears, noses, eyebrows, and, once, a penis. I could tell the penis guy had spent a lot of time on it. The spike was curved—he probably used a lighter to melt and reshape it and he had electrical tape on the ends to keep it in. I didn't make him take it out. A penis piercing wasn't a threat. It was a twisted form of hope. Keeping that hole open was him saying that he was going to leave that jail. I didn't strip him of that.

How Gorilla put it was, "This is how it works: there's a man and there's an inmate. You strip the inmate. You talk to the man." And I tried. I lifted and separated the two, pulled back any emotions. It was prophylactic. I bent with the single-stitched uniform and spread my fingers inside the gloves—filling them. Then gave commands. And talked about anything but.

Huddle Up

ONE guard said, "What's the deal?"

Eight of us stood at the gate, grouped for warmth, going on five minutes. We wore black winter coats. Department of Corrections patches all over.

Another guard said, "Let me explain the deal: who gives a shit?"

Another said, "But it's time to make a quick buck. Maybe get a haircut."

Another said, "Nah. Don't. Inmates and scissors and vital organs don't mix."

Another said, "Nah. Go ahead. They're scared. Like babies. They won't hurt you."

Another said, "Yeah. Take the haircut. Only costs a dollar. But get a white barber. Black barbers can't cut white guy hair."

The gate buzzed. We stepped through. I held the gate.

One said, "That's mighty white of you."

We split. We took posts. We took gates. We clipped keys to our belts.

Inmates walked in groups without stopping. Too cold to stop. And windy. They wore their brown corduroy jackets. DOC stenciled all over.

I stepped into the former death house. Jail court was in session. I had been summoned.

In the conference room, four new guards stood against the wall. They wore civvies still, touring the jail before heading off to the academy. Class 620. They were white and goateed. The room: wood paneled. The table: ancient. Sitting on one side: Snickers. He wore an orange jumpsuit. On the

other, the jail judge (jail speak for hearing examiner—he presided over misconduct reports and handed out consequences). He wore a suit and examined what he heard from Snickers.

Snickers pleaded, "I took a candy bar from his pocket. That's it. Just
candy."

The misconduct in question: did Snickers give another inmate a handjob during the medication line?

The judge asked, "Then why are you looking around so much on
camera?"

"It got stuck. That's why I kept pulling."

The tour guards watched Snickers squirm.

This is jail, class 620, I wanted to tell them, where all sex is a crime and
the excuses are not one bit believable.

Next stop training room.

Then mail room.

Then years and years of paid sex enforcement.

The judge found Snickers guilty of "Engaging in sexual acts with others
or sodomy." The sentence: ninety days in the bucket. Snickers clicked his
tongue. A bucket guard escorted Snickers off to begin his sentence.

Next on the docket: my misconduct. A guard walked a big inmate into
the room. The inmate's uniform: orange jumpsuit and handcuffs. He sat.
The judge read:

> I, COI Langston, served a misconduct report to inmate Bibey
> #EL3897. Upon reaching his cell, I asked for his ID card. He
> responded with, "If you call me a nigger again, I'll kill you." He
> repeated this two more times.

The judge asked if we had anything to add. We looked at each other.

I expected him to threaten me again. To accuse me again.

Instead, Bibey #EL3897 said, "I blacked out. I don't remember."

Class 620 looked from him to me.

I shrugged, surprised at his response.

The judge said, "Fine, then. I find officer Langston credible. Sixty days
in the restricted housing unit."

The judge didn't ask if I called him a nigger.

I was ready to tell him that I hadn't.

But he shuffled his papers and said, "Moving on."

A bucket officer collected Bibey and took him away.

Bibey didn't want to kill me. I was sure of it. He wanted to kill somebody else. But tickets were supposed to be short and clear even if they sacrificed the larger story. Even if that larger story is one of the largest: racism.

My part of the hearing over, I walked to the chapel, my assignment for the day. Inmates built the chapel from stone sometime in the seventies. It matched the towers.

I unlocked the door and waited for count to end. A small desk sat near the door. That was for the guard.

The chaplain, an older guy, walked in and punched me in the ribs. He said, "You better tighten up, son."

The chaplain used to be a boxer. Or that's just what people said because he beat up an inmate once. The inmate had hit him first.

Since it was Friday afternoon we had the Buddhists and general counseling. The Muslims would be in after dinner. Just three Buddhists showed up. They were young and white. They burned incense, chatted, and meditated. Two inmates stood at the desk asking about the different services, when a civilian counselor walked in. She hugged me. She had done it before. She gave occasional sermons at my childhood church. I no longer went, but that didn't stop the hugs.

It never let me be a guard when she did that. The idea was to separate home and jail life. I practiced and practiced this technique. I transitioned from medication-line handjobs to a discussion with my fiancée about whose turn it was to wash the dishes after that short drive home. In jail, it wasn't a conversation about "Why won't the landlord let us paint our walls?" It was one inmate saying to another inmate, "Suck a dick, yo, suck-a-suck-a-dick." If I thought about my fiancée while in jail, my brain went something like: nah, don't. Outside the gates, I had plans to build a Japanese arch–style TV stand. Inside I had threats on my life.

Inside was not supposed to have hugs.

The counselor took the two inmates at the desk and listed their prospects: Native American, Rastafarian, Wiccan, Muslim, Catholic, or general Christian. She explained which nights they worshipped. Their pros. She gave no cons. She offered a tour of the building.

The chaplain walked out and said, "They're just scared. Those kids. They're looking for a group to hide in. You have to choose a group."

The Buddhists left. Their hour up.

And so was mine. I had to work the meal line. The chaplain took over the desk.

The lieutenant in charge put me in dining hall 3. I took my position at the end of the rows to seat inmates. They took trays of baked chicken and macaroni. They sat where I pointed. Almost all the inmates who ate in dining hall 3 were white. The black guys mostly ate in dining hall 1. The Hispanics mostly in 2. They self-segregated all over the jail: in yard, in cellmates, in religious groups, at the barbershop.

The leader of the white supremacists walked in and looked at my feet. Then looked me in the eyes. Then gave this up-nod sort of gesture. His head shaved, of course. He was young and short and walked with his arms out. Like a gunslinger. A swastika peeking from his tank top. Seven clones followed. They got their chicken. They walked toward me.

I nodded back to the leader because I figured it was his weird way of saying hi.

His group sat where I pointed.

They belonged to the World Church of the Creator and Nazi Low Rider hate groups. Word was only oldheads belonged to the Aryan Brotherhood.

Another six hundred or so white guys filed in and filed out. Eighty-two percent of Pennsylvania is white. That's outside the gate. But inside: only 40 percent. They were minorities for the first time. Which sent many to the hate groups. Easy recruits.

I walked over to the guard at the door once the line emptied. He had his sleeves rolled under at the wrist. We weren't allowed to roll them up. This was a way around the rules. I did it too. Most did. If it was cold outside, the buildings were eighty degrees.

White guy after white guy dumped his tray and walked out into the cold. Clusters moved by outside: devil worshippers, cross-dressers, gang-bangers, Bible carriers, muscleheads, library workers, basketball players, guards.

Groups eyeballed groups.

The door guard said, "The skinheads like you. You joining up?"

He pointed at my feet. "You dress like them."

The one uniform freedom guards had was footwear. Meaning, we had to buy our own boots. They had to be black. That was the rule. Most guards chose hiking boots. I bought a black pair of Doc Martens. They were comfortable and durable. I always had a pair.

The door guard told me, "That's the skinhead boot of choice."

Shit, was all I managed to say.

Naturally I had bought the wrong footwear. The one thing I didn't copy from the guards turned out to be an inmate thing. I already couldn't grow a goatee. I was not fitting in. Some people should not be guards. I began to think this about myself.

But the blue collar doesn't care about that. The blue collar makes people take whatever they can get, good at it or not.

We ate chicken and macaroni. Ten guards at the table. We talked shoe-polish eyeliner. We talked handjobs. We debated prices. A handjob had to be cheaper than a blowjob. Had to be. We dumped trays.

~

CHAPEL was on. Muslims trickled in. They took off their shoes and pushed the pews to the side. They unrolled a room-sized carpet. Eighty guys knelt on the carpet. Only one was white. As a group they grew long beards. They rolled their pants up above the ankles. Many had calluses on their foreheads from their prayer carpets. They didn't look scared.

The imam showed up and led the service.

Then a lieutenant walked in and took me to the chaplain's office. He had white hair. He told me that inmate Bibey #EL3897 had written a grievance. He said, "Check it out, he says right here that, *COI Langston call me a nigger and spit on my face and chest.*"

He asked after a pause, "So, did you do any of that?"

The lieutenant was in charge of first-year guards. First-year guards are easy to fire. First-year guards have no union backing. First-year guards start stuttering when accused of misconduct like this.

At least that's how I responded.

I told him that I was confused when Bibey said that. Like majorly confused. I said, I've never said the word in my life. And I never spoke to that inmate before. Like not one word. I was just trying to deliver a ticket. The whole interaction, it made no sense. Like none.

The lieutenant nodded and wrote something down on the form.

He said, "Okay. I say here that I find your argument credible."

Then asked, "Hey, by the way, why did you want to be a guard?"

I began an interview answer, something about how it was a job that let you progress professionally and perform a public service at the same time but he cut me off with "I'm fucking with you. I know you're in it for the money. Why else would we be here?"

Blue-collar communion. I was thankful for it.

"You know," he said. "If you had sideburns, you would look just like the first officer who ticketed Bibey that night." He looked at me.

I said, maybe.

The lieutenant left.

The imam said, "Ameen."

Muslims came out of the sanctuary with bro-hugs and laughs. They found their shoes, rolled up the carpet, and dragged the pews back into place.

I searched the chapel from bathrooms to ceiling tiles to pray carpet to pulpit. One of the few escape attempts at Rockview involved two inmates cramming into the pulpit. It rotated around for the different religions and had a storage area for different texts. Circular salvation. Two recounts and a jail-wide search found the guys.

I locked the doors, walked the keys to the control center. The control sergeant told me to report to D block.

So I reported to D block.

From the bubble, Shrek said, "Oh, cool, how'd we get so lucky?"

I said, Hi. Close the showers, right?

"Yep. So smart. And so cute."

The shower guard I relieved was arguing with Melvin at the door. Melvin said, "It's too cold! Just turn the handle a bit."

The guard said, "Nah. Just get in there and huddle up with the others. You know, for warmth."

Melvin said, "Why you like this? Always."

Melvin still had his clothes on. His hand under the stream. He left.

The rest of the inmates showered without complaint. One smoked a cigarette.

I said, Really, dude?

He put it out.

Then we counted. The first three cells blasted rap music from their radios. Same station, like a block party. The guard with me told them, "Turn that crap down."

"Sure, boss," one of the inmates said. "This isn't for you anyway."

We walked down the range. The guard said, "This job makes you racist." He had sideburns. And he was the guard that Bibey really wanted to kill. His sleeves were rolled under at the wrist.

We did look the same.

Even if I hadn't realized it the week before when I walked up to range 4 to deliver the ticket to a big black guy who was six foot three, probably weighing 320 pounds, and wearing nothing but stained boxers. He pressed his gut against the bars. His cell light was on. His teeth were dirty, his chest hair full of crumbs. The range was dark. I smelled cigarettes and some kind of cooking meat.

The misconduct was for "Using inappropriate language with staff."

Bibey had called Sideburns a white boy fake cop, allegedly.

Melvin, next door, said, "You should give that ticket like nope."

In Bibey's cell I saw chips bags and playing cards on the floor.

I said, I have a misconduct report here for inmate Bibey #EL3897—can I see your ID card?

Melvin said, "Tear it up, CO, tear it up."

Bibey responded with "If you call me a nigger again, I'll kill you." His breath smelled like sour cream and onion.

Melvin went quiet.

I said, What?

He repeated himself slowly this time, with more onion breath.

I told him, Hold on a sec.

I found Shrek. He was delivering the inmate mail that hadn't been picked up earlier. I told him what happened. He walked up with me. Bibey leaned on the bars again and said with higher tone in his voice, "I'm serious. If you call me a nigger again, I'll kill you."

Shrek turned to me: "Well, what are you waiting for? Write him up." Then Shrek took an awkward sidestep as though he was trying to fix a wedgie without using his hands, and dragged his heels down the range to deliver the rest of the mail.

While writing the misconduct, Sideburns whispered in my ear, "Don't be a snake. Don't say nigger in it."

Which told me plenty.

I couldn't understand him. Why make jail harder than it already was?

A lieutenant came on the block to lock Bibey up until jail court. On their way out, Bibey yelled at me, "You don't know what you started!"

The lieutenant looked at me. Everyone in the bubble looked at me. In the bubble's glass, I looked at me.

~

ON chapel night, the uniform still too big. Sideburns still wearing one to match. He said, "Last time you were here, didn't you piss someone off?"

I said, Something like that. And took my place in the card game.

Shift ended. The D block crew walked in a pack. Sideburns right next to me. Not a foot between us.

I had to choose a group.

And there was only one.

We stopped at the gate.

One guard said, "It didn't smell as bad tonight."

Another said, "Nah. You just weren't talking as much."

The gate buzzed.

We scattered.

Compounded

HOW to prepare a chichi: take a potato chip bag, put in two soups. Add jail meat: maybe a gristle-filled kielbasa. Throw in anything traded from a jail cook: a pepper, an onion. Add whatever works from the commissary: cheese, maybe some Mrs. Dash Salt-Free Original Blend Seasoning. Tie the bag shut with a shoelace. Boil with a stinger in a tub of water. Open and top with crumbled chips.

~

THE ingredients could be found on the walks (jail speak for sidewalks). Hungry men tired of the compound's food traded and bartered through quick handshakes and hugs.

But the jail had an officer patrolling the walks at all times to stop it. And that was me, one Sunday, in a five-degree wind, ingredient-snatching. The quota: ten inmates to pull over, pat down, and metal-detect.

After being one of the per-policy five officers randomly patted down by another officer at the gate, and having my bladder searched (random urinalysis drug test), I pulled over the first of the day.

1. Hoarder—tall, skinny—bulging pockets.

I took his ID card, wrote down his info on the clipboard: number, name, block, destination, but left the line for "contraband" blank until the end. I put the clipboard on top of the trash can and asked him to empty his pockets onto it.

He piled mayonnaise packets, napkins, empty chip bags, plastic dining-hall forks, spoons, expired milk, shoelaces, passes, old socks, new socks, empty packs of Kite, rolling papers, and more rolling papers, and why anyone with not one strand of tobacco would collect three hundred scattered rolling papers, enough to paper the walls in his cell, was beyond me.

All Hoarder said was, "Man, man, man" when I threw most of his mayonnaise, his milk, his anything extra away.

He said, "You're too new to be thieving me."

I did, actually, still feel new.

On the clipboard, once clear, in the contraband box, I wrote, *Dining hall cutlery: 6 spoons, 5 forks.* Hoarder stepped back into the wash of inmates.

Those lawbreakers grouped together for warmth and breathed out a cloud of steam.

2. Melvin—short, serious—kicking a ball of paper.

I really just wanted to talk to him.

I asked how things were going.

He said, "No one has hit me yet."

So that's good, right?

"No, dummy, just no one has hit me yet."

I asked for his ID card.

"Lost it, dummy."

I regretted pulling him over.

That's okay, I told him, I know your name and number. Turn around please.

I squeezed the back of his jacket and felt a big lump. I made him take the jacket off.

"Okay, dummy."

The walks were mostly clear. A yard guard watched me from the yard gate. He had a scarf up to his eyes.

I dug around in Melvin's jacket for the best interest of the compound. The lump: twelve pieces of bread wrapped in a paper towel.

He said, "For my PBJs, dummy."

I never knew how strict to roll. Guards with time in said to roll hard. It's an easier walk.

Even the Code of Ethics handbook given at graduation seemed to say the same thing, with thirty-nine specific rules covering the use of profanity to fraternization with inmates. And it came with a warning. Section C says, "Any employe who violates the provisions of this code shall be subject to immediate disciplinary action . . ."

"Employee" spelled like that is a corporate thing. One "e" saves ink, therefore saves money. The corporate-y handbook made me a bit paranoid. But this was Melvin. And I just wanted to talk, not decide whether to enforce a petty rule or not. Was letting him keep the bread fraternization?

In two years I would be strapping him down to a bunk with heavy leather restraints without any internal debate.

But this was still early. And I confiscated his bread. I didn't want to violate the code—plus the yard guard was eyeballing me. I had to. I said sorry and meant it.

Melvin said, "No, you not, dummy."

So, let the record show, I did the right thing: I protected the walks from Melvin's alleged peanut butter and jelly sandwiches.

And felt like a dummy for it.

3. Emphysema—big smile, used a walker.

He had a pocket full of cigarette butts. He said, "Old ones, CO. Don't smoke no more." He was dying the entire time I dressed up for Rockview. The nurses banned him from buying commissary tobacco on account of his terminal lung disease, but he scoured the walks for butts.

He shivered. The yard guard walked over and said, "It gets colder here than anywhere else in the state. It's the wind. It's the empty fields and concrete." I couldn't tell who he was. He had a mustard stain where his name tag should have been. That was a code violation according to section B-12: "Employes in uniform are required to keep said uniforms in a clean and neat condition."

Emphysema shivered again.

Winter for me as a kid was the hill across the street. If we had snow, I was on it until dark. We had rules:

1) No walking up the middle.
2) No runner sleds on the jump (tears up the jump).
3) No braking with heels (tears up the slope).
4) Fix what you tear up.

There's a right way to do everything, according to the consensus. For sledding, for jail, for life. And it's natural to police. Classes on slope procedures were short and direct. I hit an older kid with my runner sled on purpose. He dared to walk up the middle. He kicked me in the stomach. I threw him down. And all the hill cops ran over to break it up.

Emphysema picked up a butt from the snow. Even though he was dying from it, he still smoked, never yielded. Not an unusual personality trait in jail.

Emphysema's rules:

1) Self-destruct.
2) Self-destruct.
3) Self-destruct.

I didn't confiscate his life story. He walkered away.

4. Oldhead—big gut, big gray beard.

When I popped his collar and ran my hands through his armpits, he asked, "Why you here, young buck?"

I said, Money, and squatted down to feel his pants' seams.

I asked what brought him to Rockview?

"Same thing," he said. "Armed robbery."

My radio interrupted us. The control center called, "Corner officers, cover the corners for the return of the yard."

The four corners of the walks had to be manned during major line movements: yard, meal, chapel, education, work, and medication. Compound Patrol's corner was the one outside of the Special Needs Unit, the block for the mentally challenged.

The radio talked the walks all shift:

"Corner officers, cover your corners."

"Are the walks covered?"

"Are the walks clear?"

"We got B block on the walks."

"C block coming around."

And over the radio, I called out my responses,

Covered.

Clear.

Covered.

The radio called, "A Yard on the walks." The inmates flocked to the gate. The guard had trouble unlocking it. The inmates called out, "Turn the key. Turn the key. Turn the key."

I ran the handheld metal detector over Oldhead's chest. "I don't play no more," he said. The detector beeped at his navel. He lifted his jacket to show me his belt buckle. "I don't play no more," he said again. "Tickets mess with your money." He was talking about jail jobs—inmates lose them if written up. Then there was no commissary, no chichis, and no Mrs. Dash for whatever meatish meat served next meal. He only had his ID card and library pass. Traveling light. Traveling right.

5. George—nicotine-stained fingers, liver spots.

He hung out at the commissary corner. I walked by and said hello. He asked, "When do you retire?"

My answer was that I had just started. I asked when he was.

He said, "I'll retire when I expire," then watched for my reaction. He was a lifer. Rockview had two hundred of them, one in ten guys. I wasn't really sure what to say. I think he thought it was funny, my pause, then said, "Nice clipboard. You going to pat me down?"

Instead I stopped a young guy who spit only two feet away from my boot. He had a stinger in his jacket. I told him his misconduct report would show up later.

I didn't write it. Just wanted to sweat him for spitting near me.

6. Aggravator—scar on his right cheek.

Me: Step over here for a second.

Him: You need to put on new gloves.

Me: These are fine.

Him: Would you use the same condom more than once?

Me: Turn around, please.

Him: Why choose me?

Me: Spread your legs.

Him: Damn, man.

Me: More. Spread them.

Him: Come on. You're a tourist here. I live this.

Me: Do it right.

Me again: And do it right now.

Him: Give me a grievance.

Me: Talk to your block sergeant about that.

I headed into the education building to warm up. That building had benches, classrooms, a bathroom, and an oldhead guard sitting at a desk. He had forty inmate ID cards on top. One from each guy in the building.

He said, "New, right? Don't use vacation your first year. Or they'll can you. And wash your hands. A lot. Need some numbers for your sheet?" He pushed the ID cards at me.

I said, Tempting, but no thanks, and resumed my search for grievances.

7. Head chef—old.

He had a plastic bag sticking out of his pocket. I didn't pat him down, just pulled the bag out. In it, four raw burgers. He was a dining-hall cook.

Chef said, "I'm on chichi duty tonight. Six of us go in together. Special for the game. It's about the interplay of spices. The way the palate informs the pleasure center in the brain." Then he said, "I'm joking. It's about the meat. I really need it. Otherwise it's dogshit."

I threw it in the trash.

He shrugged and said, "The nachos won't be the same. But hey, I gotta feed the warden" (jail speak for take a dump). He hacked a hacky cough and walked away.

I patrolled. Inmates eyeballed me. I drafted close behind two other cooks leaving the dining hall.

One told the other that he lost his wife and two daughters the year before. They died in a car wreck. He was at Rockview when it happened.

Their pockets looked flat. I let them go.

And that was important.

It wasn't my empathy that let them go, it was their flat pockets—dead daughters need not apply. I was proud of the callousness. My goal: to hone that walk. No more invasive hesitations. No more dummy.

8. Loam—filth.

He had dried food on his gut and sleeves. Food flaked off and snagged my gloves when I ran my hands down his chest. I ended the search and was about to order Loam to wash his jacket but my radio yelled, "Officer needs assistance in BA block!"

So I handed Loam his ID card and assisted.

9. Colin—muscly, dead.

He was gray. He used to be black. He lay on a top bunk, wearing white boxers and vomit.

I should not have responded.

Not because it was an ugly scene, but because I was supposed to be covering my corner. Section B-8 states, "No employe shall leave his assigned post without being properly relieved." The call could have been anything though, an assault on staff—I figured the walks could stay straight without me for thirty seconds.

Four guards took the corners of his mattress, and I got underneath to lift with my shoulders and back. It was hot. Chichis roasted. I had on my jacket, neck warmer, earmuffs, and hat.

Out on the range, on the floor, the block guard began CPR. A nurse showed up and took over and while I watched Colin's muscly chest compressing down, I remembered that he was the guy who always brought a bottle of hot sauce with him to the dining hall. Down for rape. I heard that he was one of the innocent ones—after twelve years he had been cleared by DNA and was waiting for his walking papers. The state was making amends by restitution.

The guards took turns saying, "He's gone."

I said it too.

Free-world paramedics drove an ambulance right up to the block. Standard procedure. I helped load the stretcher. We cuffed the body to it.

A jail nurse said heart attack. I wrote the body's name and number on the clipboard.

10. I made up the last name and number.

Because people were dying around me and for ten minutes I stopped caring about their fucking pockets.

Callous no more.

Then my patrol finished.

Then I met my replacement in the education building. He took the stack of inmate ID cards from the desk, filled his sheet, then stood and said, "I'm going out to E block to feed the warden."

Months earlier, I had discovered that officer sitting on the back steps of A block eating an extra-cheesy chichi with a chow-hall spoon. The spoon had probably been used for many purposes by the inmate who made him breakfast. The guard offered me some.

Section B-6 of the code states, "There shall be no fraternization or private relationship of staff with inmates. . . . This includes, but is not limited to, trading, bartering or receiving gifts."

I said I wasn't hungry but thanks.

It was 8 a.m.

Disgusted, definitely.

But you can do everything right: refuse chichi gifts, confiscate bread from kids, and things can still go wrong.

Proof was on that cold, Sunday compound patrol. On the way to the dining hall, walking past the butt-free corner of the Special Needs block, I saw Chichi Guard shaking the hand of Oldhead, the "I don't play no more" armed robber. They stood by the commissary. And when their hands separated, Oldhead put his hand into his pocket suspiciously like the guard had passed him something. They saw me coming, gave each other a guilty look, and Oldhead ducked into the block.

Then it was just me and Chichi Guard looking at each other.

Section B-14 of the handbook states, "Employes will promptly report to their supervisor any information which comes to their attention and indicates violation of the law."

He asked, "How are the walks?"

I said, Square.

He said, "Well, enjoy them." And walked toward E.

I watched him go.

What I should have done was follow Oldhead, turn out his pockets, and see what he had. Yes, Chichi would have called me a snitch and ruined my career if it was nothing but a ketchup packet or shoelace. And yes, if it turned out to be drugs, or a cell phone, that guard would have been given a chance to resign and I would still be called the snitch, the no-good snitch. Chichi had time in. He had friends. Who cares if inmates use drugs?

So I did nothing and got to be complicit.

And for the rest of my time at Rockview, Chichi sat by me in the dining hall and invited me into card games.

He shook my hand.

This compounded everything.

The handbook says report, report, report. But what it really needs is a section D, a recipe for the sting of it all. Something like . . .

HOW to prepare an employee for jail: take a man-mash packed into a compound with hoarding, self-destruction, aggravation, crust, heart pains, sneaky handshakes—an original blend—and stew it in six-by-nine-by-too-fucking-close-to-other-men-feeding-the-warden cells and not stimulate the pleasure center of the brain. Even in a cold, fresh winter wind, prepare to be unprepared. Learn the helplessness. When you see a guard violating the code, needlessly making your job more difficult, don't worry, if by chance that asshole goes down, it'll be a courtesy flush. But don't expect it. And in the meantime, because of your inaction, you get to feel like a dummy. This could last your entire career. Bring to a boil. Top with crumbled chips.*

* This tastes like dogshit.

Breaking Things

MELVIN dragged his mattress down the range. I stepped on it.

"Yo!" he yelled.

I asked him where he was going.

He said, "I'ma throw it over the fence and climb that mother to freedom."

I asked if I should report his plan.

He said, "You should if you's a bitch."

Put it back, I said.

He did.

And I went and found a mechanic-turned-double-murderer on the block. Word was he used a compound bow to end a love triangle. My car shook when I hit the brakes. I told him that. He had two teardrop tattoos under his eye and advice. "The rotors, they warp over time. Replace them." That sounded good. He seemed trustworthy. He also told me, "And you have to talk to Melvin like a kid. Because that's what he is. A kid."

That night I took the rear wheels off and started cranking. But the first rotor wouldn't let go. I pried hard. Next came out the hammer and yep, that did it. The rotor popped off. But it came with a small explosion of springs. Turns out I had left the emergency brake on. That's what had broken.

I asked myself then, as I always have in those moments, what have I done?

The car's back end rested on two jacks in the parking lot. I sat on the curb. The disassembly happened the week after carrying the dead man then driving home to tell my fiancée nothing about it. I had turned on a video game instead. And wished the drive was longer.

I called my father. Mortality, a car on two jacks, the upcoming marriage, these had me shaky. I didn't tell him the specifics, just touched on the strangeness of my place.

He's a scientist who typically looks for the logic in situations. And he asked then as he always has, "Why do you do these things?"

He meant: why take *that* job.

But he asked me the same thing senior year when a police officer sent me home after catching me skipping class.

And a few weeks later when the police informed him that I received tickets for criminal trespass and criminal mischief for being a dumbass teen.

He asked when I joined the army.

And after a bunch of speeding tickets.

And when I took the Melvin-inspired job teaching at-risk boys.

And more recently when I took a job at the hospital to keep homicidal and suicidal patients safe.

Why do you do these things?

~

A WRITING mentor once told me that I lived an ephemeral life, the way I switched jobs.

After looking up the word "ephemeral" I agreed.

In each new job, the first year is full of wonder.

The second, you master it.

The third, drudgery and boredom and time to move on. At least for me. During graduate school I loaded trucks at night. The ceiling of the warehouse consisted entirely of conveyors. It shook and rolled boxes nonstop. Occasionally a pickle or mayonnaise jar fell, sending everyone running. The conveyors streamed thousands of boxes down to the loaders. We handpacked our trucks. The loader in the next lane wrote on the wall of each trailer to see if he would get the same truck again. His message to himself:

YOU ARE THE BOXMAN

He saw me staring at the conveyors and said, "Come worship at the altar of capitalism" and helped me throw a plastic pool on top of boxes of toilet paper, bleach, candy bars, and pimple cream. "Us loaders," he said. "We carry all the world's shit."

I'm never immune to the first-year surprise of it all. That insider look into heavy worlds. Problem is, the feeling never lasts.

On one end of the jail's bunker, at night, thousands of worms poked their heads out of the hill. It was their shadows I saw first while I walked the fence, inspecting it for anything out of place. The jail's lights made for a nightlong sunset, and the shadows disappeared in waves. At first I thought something was running, a plague of mice maybe, or a cloud of bats, until I moved closer and saw those worms sucking back into their holes. They rustled as the one or two inches of them exposed to the night air contracted for protection or whatever they were doing—planning the next uprising maybe. Only on that hill have I seen worms like that, and only at night. The wind brought me the sounds of the chapel choir working the men into a frenzy. The bass player shook everything.

The contrast: in an unremarkable classroom a few miles away and a few years earlier a lightweight professor had asked me, "You don't know what a tilde is? How did you make it through admissions?"

An unbearable world. I'd rather load a truck. Strip a man.

I told him I paid the fifty-dollar application fee.

And that the little wavy line looked like barbed wire.

And that I liked to use it for section breaks in my papers.

He said, "That's not what it's for."

~

I TOOK the drivable car in. My fiancée said, "Treat it nice."

I rattled the gate and manned my post: a seat in a bubble with four buttons that opened doors. My purpose that day: to check passes like some kind of hall-pass monitor for inmates going to doctor appointments.

THE BUTTONMAN

Melvin came through and said, "No to the pass. No to the ID. No to the drugs. No to the goddamn cops."

And I laughed—everything was unexpected with him—which made him laugh.

He had cereal boxes on his feet (Frosted Flakes, the single-serving boxes). He said, "Someone ganked my shoes." I got him to show me his pass: a psychiatrist appointment. Which explained the drug talk: behavior modifiers, no doubt. He clomped down the hallway.

Then a stocky guard stopped to talk to me. I appreciated that. I always had questions for the more experienced. But he said, "It's because of fucking guys like you that I can't wear my hat. Open the outside door." I opened the door after a pause. He stomped through. Those were the first and last words he ever said to me.

I had bought a less trucker-looking hat that turned blue after one month of sun, rain, and snow. Apparently he had one just like it, but his sergeant had made him get rid of it. His was still black. He worked mostly indoors, but his sergeant wanted his block officers to dress by the code.

A month later a lifer shattered Hat Guard's cheekbone and elbow with a mop handle. The mop handle broke and the lifer stabbed him with the splintered end. Hat took a leave of absence, which turned into permanent absence.

My hat, that's what he was worried about. My hat.

~

AND I walked onto D block a few days later, my car still on jacks and waiting for the parts, to Melvin screaming at his celly, "I ain't scared of it or you or him or no one!"

His celly said to me, "You better get him away from me."

I got Melvin on the range. I asked, Why are you doing this?

He said, "'Cause I'm not scared!"

Well, yeah, but what about?

"He's lying. Says I'm scared of water."

Melvin's fingernails were dirt-packed. Crusted nose. Blanket lint in his hair. A piece of tape hanging from his elbow. White T-shirt, more brown T-shirt.

His celly wanted him to bathe.

I asked him when was the last time he took a shower.

He said, "You can't make me" and ran out with the inmates to the yard.

He should not have been in jail. Clear to anyone.

And a day later Melvin cried after lying to a block guard about having a library pass when he didn't have one, which made him say to the guard, "I'll kill myself if you write me up," which made the guard report him to Control, which made Control report him to the psychiatric staff, who responded by collecting Melvin and putting him in an observation cell to be continually monitored so he wouldn't kill himself. But first they made him shower.

It took an entire jail just to get him to wash.

What would it take to repair his childhood trauma?

~

I PIECED the emergency brake together with the help of online manuals. It was just a machine. Easy. Replace the rotten and worn parts. Hit the gas. You're good.

But I was at the jail six months, and while the jail handbook talked rules and passes, there was nothing about how to correct. At least not in a meaningful way.

I wanted the satisfaction of a perfectly packed trailer. A new rotor.

Instead, what jail streamed to me was a nonstop conveyor of tests.

I stepped onto D block and hustlers stepped to me.

The first: "Man, I would kill for some ChapStick. Cherry flavor. I dream of that stuff. Look at my lips."

Rough. Sorry, man.

You aren't lying. "What could I do to get you to bring some in for me?"

Nothing, sorry.

Then next guy who wanted to talk: "What I need is a paper. Lord, please, just the sports section. Last week's will work. You get the paper at home?"

Um, no.

And the next: "Hey, CO. You seem cool. I feel like I can talk to you. Any chance I can get some reading glasses from you? Just a cheap pair. I'll end it all if I can't see my daughter's photo clear-like. Or, better yet, can I get a lighter off you so I can fix my broken ones? I'll just melt them back together. See where they broke? When Pops died, Moms lost her mind at the funeral. He didn't have his glasses on in the casket. 'It's not him!' she screamed. 'It's not him!' The whole funeral went to shit until I drove home to get his glasses. And they still had his fingerprints on them. And what do you do, clean them off? Clean off your dead pops's fingerprints? Would you? But you see, right? You see how much I need that lighter?"

All I managed for him was a "Wow," because I was pretty sure I had seen a version of that scenario in a movie once. But said sorry about his glasses. And said sorry about his father. Especially his father. But I couldn't bring him glasses. And I wouldn't get him a lighter. Sorry. Sorry. Sorry.

Then the murdering mechanic came around the corner. He asked, "Replace those rotors?"

Yeah, perfect, thanks for the advice.

"Told you," he said. "So what are you going to give me? That information ain't free."

Then he asked, "How about a lighter?"

~

THAT night I told my fiancée that they tried me. Like nonstop. But at least the car drove right. After dinner she put out a scented candle and asked, "Could you hand me the lighter."

Then gave a confused look.

And I slowly fixed my face. Apparently it twisted.

"What was that?"

I didn't know, I said. Heartburn maybe.

~

LAST day that week I found Melvin during my lunch break. His suicide-watch cell didn't have a mattress. I told him through the glass, "Let's get you right. Let's play a game. Ever play I Spy?"

This was going to work. Kids loved that game. He walked to the window.

I'll start, I said. I spy with my little eye somebody tough.

Melvin said, "I spy a bitch. I spy a bitch. A bitch! A bitch! A bitch! A bitch! . . ."

WHAT had I done?

Without Control, It Could Get Criminal

SUPER Bowl Sunday I worked the control center. Control was the ultimate beat for a motivated young guard trying to prove that I was, at least, motivated.

When the lieutenant, an obese man with a blond mustache, called my name at roll call, a guard standing next to me asked, "Whose kid are you?" (Kid is jail speak for brown nose, or pet.)

But when I walked into the control center, the regulars—the captain, the lieutenant, the old sergeant, and the two stocky goateed guards—collectively asked, "Who are you and what are you doing here?"

They were all from the same town, a forty-five-minute drive away and known for its diaper factory. They graduated from the same high school. They carpooled. It was a club. Not that they were bad guys. Just related, probably.

A Goatee put me on the doors. I controlled them with a podium that had twenty switches and lights. He said, "You can't fuck up. Only one door will open at a time."

For my first few months at Rockview, the control center was in the physical center of the jail, in the former execution house. But Control was decentralized in case of an inmate revolution and moved to the treatment building. There, on the edge of the compound, it was safer, stronger, and air-conditioned. Downstairs, through two doors, past one guard bubble, through two more doors, and inside yet another safety-glass bubble, I flipped switches. The doors didn't buzz, they popped and clicked.

A line of officers came down behind me to get radios and keys and jobs. The sergeant handed out the jobs to the rare extra guards: yard, E block, any block. Obese Lieutenant left to lock up a problem inmate. He said, "It's too early for this." The captain shuffled papers—everyone called him Grace. He seemed tense. He kept standing to pull up his pants. He ran his fingers through his hair.

He was a jail success story. Worked his way through the chain link from trainee to shift commander. I wondered what it took.

Physically, it looked like another hundred pounds.

He put his hand on my shoulder and asked, "So, what brings you here? No school for you? You talk like you should be in school. You try the highway patrol? There is freedom in the highway patrol. The young and bright should be in the highway patrol. Or in school. Not in it here."

I told him that I tried school. He nodded.

"Married?"

Engaged.

"Going to have kids right away?"

Yes.

"Her idea?"

Also yes.

"Yeah. Look now. Listen: jailcops divorce at a higher rate than the public. They kill themselves twice as much too. They talk all day but don't communicate. You feel me?"

This is what I could feel. The strong grip of almost thirty years inside.

~

THE inmates were still locked down from count on first shift. The diaper-factory guards talked numbers—seventeen kitchen workers, eight laundries, two boiler houses, twenty-three visits—and decided that, yes, we had them all.

One of the Goatees picked up the radio. "Control to all areas, count is clear. Yard out."

Somebody radioed back, "Make that ten more minutes."

Somebody else radioed, "Make that fifteen."

Somebody else radioed, "Make that never. Keep 'em locked up."

That was the standard radio banter that filled each shift. It didn't seem to bother the control-center family.

And for the first two hours, at all times, someone stood at one of the doors waiting to get in or out. I ran visitors through the metal detector. An elderly couple showed up too late. We turned them away. They came from Philadelphia, a three-hour drive.

One officer ran the radios. Another the phones. Another the key room. A guard on steroids walked through and said, "Side door." He wanted into the visiting room. I popped the stairs by accident. He said, "Try again, young buck" while walking over to slam it shut. I got it the second time.

Turtle—a slow-moving but friendly guard—stood at the stairwell door. I almost didn't see him. He kind of hid behind the frame. I popped him in. He walked over to the window, his pants sagging, and said, "I'm extra today. I guess I need a job."

The sergeant said, "Where you been?"

Turtle said, "First I went to yard, but no, and then I went to E building, but they had three guys already, and then—"

The sergeant cut him off. "Go sit in Tower 4 until I decide what to do with you."

Turtle looked excited and stopped by the key room.

To me, the sergeant said, "That fucking guy."

I popped that fucking guy out once he got Tower 4's key.

~

JAIL control is a group of people who take payment to support a system. The system of control is more important than the actual bars. And this is why: that day, with me popping doors, Rockview's inmate capacity was 1,700, but we had 2,096 inmates discussing whether or not it was too cold to hit the yard. And to control them, we had only about eighty staff members on shift. And here's the thing: about 2,000 of the inmates—the ones not in the bucket—were free to roam all day except for two counts, which took about an hour each. Sure, on the larger blocks guards locked inmate doors after each line movement, but the inmates had the chance to step in or out every thirty minutes. On the smaller blocks, like CA, with a measly 200 inmates, the doors were open all day unless the inmate padlocked it himself. But the inmates, they surrendered to the Rockview routine. Control is a pyramid scheme that actually works.

Goal: compliance.

Start with: a control center paid to make calls.

Next with: ten sergeants paid to pass on those calls.

Followed by: sixty guards paid to enforce those calls with tickets.

And finally with: a country's worth of ticket enforcement from bucket time to five-man-goon-squad hugs to state police visits to National Guard night raids complete with bullets.

THAT call's been made.

There's always another, broader level. This is known. And this is what keeps people from resisting (too hard).

Bars just set the mood.

~

I POPPED the front door. The doctor left. Followed by the librarian. The phone rang and rang. The control center's radio call sign was 748. That was also its phone number. The 911 of the jail. In Rockview's fast-twitch world, phones required just three numbers. Three buttons from any phone got you talking to Grace, or the kitchen, or CA block, or Tower 4 just to hang up on Turtle, banished there for caring too little about his piece of the pyramid.

The control center ran the jail with those fast-dial phones. One call from Control with one voice made the entire population move. That voice was the All Call. It rang every phone at once with distractions: medical or library, yard or education, chapel or work, count or clear, anything or everything to keep the men busy. The All Call might as well have just said this: do something because doing something is better than sitting around and thinking, This is jail and this sucks. The All Call was smart. One hundred years of Rockview correcting turned it into an efficient, man-moving, all-jail ringing in our ears. There was no escaping the All Call. It rang and rang.

The sergeant handled the All Call. It was a quiet process, just a guy picking up a phone and saying a few words. "Stand by for the return of the yard."

But in the concrete blocks every phone rang, guards announced, block bells clanged, and inmates reacted.

Then the same call went across the radio, "748 to all blocks, stand by for the return of the yard."

Somebody radioed back, "Keep 'em."

Somebody else radioed a fart.

Somebody else radioed, "I concur with the previous statements."

~

A SHERIFF'S van brought us six new inmates. An ambulance took another one away. A medical supply guy delivered a tub of chemical control (pills). An angry mother called. A desperate wife called. Three guards sliced the next day already (jail speak for called off). Grace took those. The lieutenant worked on next day's roll-call sheet. He said, "Back to the blocks for you, Langston." Count was All-Called. Count was verified. A Goatee radioed, "748 to all blocks, count is clear."

Somebody radioed back, "Tell us something we don't know."

Somebody else radioed, "And thank you for your service."

Somebody else radioed, "And hold the onions."

For some reason, the cooks put onions in the tomato soup.

I popped and clicked. The perimeter's replacement walked out. The replaced perimeter walked in brushing off snow. It was wet and heavy. The sergeant sent him to D block as extra. That meant he'd patrol block out— that space between the wall and the cage with its bolted-down tables. He'd get to watch the game.

A Goatee radioed, "748 to all blocks, night yard canceled on account of the weather."

Somebody radioed back, "Imagine that."

Somebody else radioed, "What a revelation."

Somebody else radioed, "Onions? I mean, really? Onions?"

Grace left to talk an inmate down from resisting the system. The sergeant put the Super Bowl on a security monitor that had been wired with cable. He flipped it back to the security feed when Grace came back. Snow came down heavier. Grace had succeeded in talking the inmate down. No need for the goon squad.

He said, "Langston, if you want an easy life here, you gotta talk to them. Even if you don't feel like it. Even if you want to choke them out instead."

Got it, sir.

A Goatee said, "That doubles as marriage advice too. You're welcome."

Right, thanks.

Tickets came in, two from D block—hand delivered straight to Grace. He said, "Melvin again. He called Shrek a cunt. Unbelievable. I'll lock that little dude up again. Give him a timeout. I used to like him. I really did." About the second ticket Grace said, "And we need to get Mathews out of that block." He paced while reading. He wiped his glasses and called D block. He told Shrek, "He's playing the game wrong." Mathews was notorious for writing inmates up. Had hundreds to his name. He rarely made it a shift without writing two. I found him hard to talk to. He was too serious.

The lieutenant said, "I'll put him in a tower tomorrow. Him and Turtle."

Typically, our tired and used-up guards took those jobs. If a younger officer was in a tower, he was in trouble. Writing up too many inmates, or too few, or slicing a holiday got a guard in a tower for the weekend. It was punishment. Control. Inmates got the bucket. Guards got the pedestal. Both of them solitary confinement.

Grace left again. The game came on.

Few people came down the stairs then. The visiting room had long been closed. A nurse walked through to use the visiting-room vending machines. She looked at me and said, "Who are you?" I popped the door.

I told her, Newish.

I flipped through the stack of tickets. Mathews wrote the inmate up for asking him, "Why you act so tough?"

~

I WROTE an inmate up every few weeks. One guy wouldn't sit where I wanted him in the dining hall. Another for not standing for count a third time in a week. Another for sitting in his neighbor's cell. Another for screaming, "Fuck you!" when I slammed his door. He didn't even wait for me to step away, just did it right in my face—through the bars. That one made me angry. It was the first time I got mad in uniform. I told him, You bought that one. And, Enjoy the bucket. And, Right in my face? I mean-mugged him.

Control shouldn't be emotional. It'd be nice if robots ran corrections. At the water factory we had a laser with a pneumatic punch that kicked off the bottles with no caps. If it saw a flaw, it corrected. Simple. No debate. No taunting or ill will.

I felt like writing up more guys that night. But everyone else stayed away from me.

~

GRACE must have found a good place to relax. He had been gone for forty-five minutes. We watched the second quarter of the game uninterrupted. The other guards gathered around the monitor. I watched from the podium. They talked about broken legs and how they looked in slow motion. The sergeant said, "It's like it's waving hello."

A Goatee radioed, "748 to corner officers, cover your corners."

Somebody radioed back, "You see that leg?"

Somebody else radioed, "Like week-old spaghetti."

Somebody else radioed, "What?"

A Goatee radioed, "748 to all areas, prepare for the return of the gym and education building."

Somebody radioed back, "Prepared."

Somebody else radioed, "Good lookin' out."

Somebody else radioed, "So, like, they edumacated now?"

The sergeant All-Called.

Men moved.

~

EVEN though it was the Super Bowl and snowing, the programs—the schooling, the gym time—had to be held. That's part of control. Inmates expected to hit the gym. Or the chapel. They grieved if it didn't happen.

A stack of grievances sat on the counter.

The instructions read, *Provide a brief, clear statement of your grievance. State all the relief that you are seeking.*

One inmate wrote, *Relieve me from these goddamn onions.*

Another: *Where the women at?*

Another: *Them cops. All of em.*

Another: *The violation of rights at the hands of CO Mathews who been coming down on me for no reason, rubbing me down, talking to me, looking at me. He said hi three times in one shift. Clearly he plotting . . .*

The lieutenant said, "Langston, focus on the doors. Those aren't for you."

I said that the onion guy had a point.

He said, "Doors."

~

THE control center was quality control. We didn't have robots, but it seemed that a lazy human was the next-closest thing. Typically, the Turtles of the jail were too lazy to abuse their power. They didn't have sneaky handshakes, because, really, who had the energy for drug smuggling? They didn't want promotions. They didn't racially insult other humans. They wanted to do their time and get paid. Turtle had longevity. He might never burn out. I saw the benefit of Turtle's role. Even respected it.

The guards who cared too much, the Mathewses of the jail, they seemed unhealthy. But I felt pulled that way, caring about it all. Yes, it seemed stressful, but the one time I got pissed, the inmates left me alone. That was positive reinforcement for my behavior. I saw the benefit in that too.

But both Turtle and Mathews had to spend a week in a tower. So, according to the lieutenant, they were doing it wrong. Too extreme.

Somewhere between them, I guess, made you control center material.

Or you grew up near the diaper factory.

The game was one-sided and uninteresting. The diaper guards spent the rest of the night talking about high school wrestling. Their school had a long history of beating mine. They let me know it. Many times.

And the radio went, "Grace to 748."

I looked at the radio. The other guys were focused on a Goatee reliving a double-leg takedown.

Grace called again, "Grace to 748."

I told them that Grace was calling.

The sergeant said, "Then answer it."

I radioed, *Go ahead, Captain.*

And he radioed back, "Who is this?"

And that was a good question.

Goon Types

THERE are three types of men in the world, and they are all on the goon squad.

Little goons: they fight to get on the squad because of their vinegar—vinegar is a by-product of testosterone.

Big goons: they avoid the squad but are forced on anyway because of their stuff—stuff is a 46-plus-inch chest, or the ability to fight.

Temporary goons: they don't have enough daily vinegar or stuff but fill in for the little and big goons when needed (any man can be a temporary goon).

The "goon squad" is the unofficial name for a corrections emergency response team (CERT). Another, unofficial name is the evil ninja turtles. This is an inmate-given name. It references the bulky, shell-like, black body armor the team members, or goons, wear during cell extractions.

Officially, the goon squad is made up of corrections officers.

Officially.

And the goon squad upholds the will of the jail. It is the strong arm of the laws of man. A strong arm is needed because, according to the laws of nature, the probability of two thousand men stacked and locked in one concrete compound fully obeying the laws of man is zero.

In a vacuum, the acceleration of gravity is 9.8 meters per second squared for any object: a feather, a cigarette, a man who knocked a cigarette out of another man's hand. In a space devoid of free-moving air, men agitate. This is any packed bar in any town on any Friday night. This is a hot metro train in Paris. This is jail.

For a good goon squad, only the big-goon type is needed—and an agitator to bring them together. The agitator is an inmate who is usually doing time in the bucket for previous agitation. An agitator's previous agitation can take the shape of a hand-rolled lumpy cigarette worth 'round about three cents and the resulting fight over the bump that dislodged it.

An agitator has much in common with a goon squad member. This is because both are men.

Agitators are usually the little-goon type: immature and pissed off. Rarely are they the big-goon type: experienced in the ways of the world and knowing that violence only hurts. But sometimes they are the big-little-goon type, with lots of stuff and a whole lot of vinegar because they had a shit week.

A shit week can begin with a brother killed in the line of mire. Home or street life that has gone awry and left only a jail counselor to break the news, "Your brother was shot and killed." [Pause] "You don't need to talk about it, do you?" Then a lumpy cigarette rolled on the block to try and cope. Then a fight over that lumpy cigarette when shoulders knocked. Which equaled a trip to the bucket. Which meant only one phone call a week. Which meant more agitation. Which manifested itself as six straight hours of kicking on a cell door. Which necessitated the goon squad.

But this is only an example.

Usually, an agitator agitates over something small, like a four-ounce cup of leftover peanut butter from lunch that he does not want to return to the guards working the bucket. So the bucket guards call in the goons to retrieve it.

And the goons retrieve it because they are paid to.

It is important to remember that the retrieval is not about the four ounces of peanut butter. It is about enforcing the laws of man.

The proceedings begin with a lieutenant negotiating with the agitator. A temporary-type goon, or little-goon hopeful, will videotape the proceedings. Here, in essence, is the negotiation:

The lieutenant says to the agitator, "Comply."

The agitator says, "No."

The lieutenant says to the goons, "Pepper him."

The goons pepper-spray the agitator.

The lieutenant says to the agitator, "Comply."

The agitator says, "No."

The lieutenant says to the goons, "Gas him."

The goons teargas the agitator.

The lieutenant says to the agitator, "Comply."

The agitator says, "No."

The lieutenant says to the goons, "Rigorously enter the cell and make him comply."

The goons rigorously enter the cell with shackles and cuffs and vinegar and stuff.

Much of this negotiation can be nonverbal. For example, the word "no" can take the shape of an agitator's penis displayed and shaken at the goon squad and lieutenant.

Again, all of this is on video, of course, so the goons are justified for all that rigorous entering.

The use of force escalates quickly in jail. It moves from a show of force to the use of firearms in five steps. The goon squad falls under step four: active countermeasures.

The largest active-countermeasuring goon enters the agitator's cell first. He is the shield goon. The shield is the electrified hand of the strong arm of the law. Take a fifty-five-gallon drum without a lid or base, and halve it. That is the size and shape of the shield. Concave side facing out, it cups the agitator when placed correctly during the active countermeasures. The loud clicking it makes sounds like a car's windshield being driven eighty miles per hour through a hailstorm.

Really, though, the clicking is one hundred thousand volts.

Four other goons follow the shield goon into the agitator's cell, single file, moving fast, pushing all the while. The videotaping goon and lieutenant stay outside.

The four goons following the shield goon into the cell are the limb goons. When the shield goon jams the inmate against the wall or floor or bunk or ceiling or light fixture or toilet or that small little space between the bunk and back wall with his click, click, clicking shield, the limb goons grab limbs. Not a specific arm or leg—they are assigned a quadrant, like upper right or lower left. Whatever happens to be sticking out from behind the shield is what they grab. The lower left limb goon might end up with the agitator's neck.

On the way in, the shield goon must be mindful of trip lines made of sheets, and of the concrete floor, which might be soapy and slippery from a flooded toilet. These are common obstacles. Also, the door might not open all the way on account of all the trash wedged into it.

The agitator will probably be behind his mattress to take the blow. The blow needs to be as hard as goonly possible. The shield should be driven at no less than top speed with a combined weight of no less than half a ton of collective goon.

The formula for a cell extraction is force equals mass times acceleration. It can be measured in newtons, or sutures, or seconds the agitator is unconscious and lying in the soapy water.

Word problems for goons work like this: If five men with vinegar and stuff stand in a hallway waiting for the word "Go," and another man stands in a concrete cube saying over and over, "You pussies won't try me," how quickly will the goons deliver the blow?

The answer: three sprinting steps after "Go."

Initiation to the goon squad involves the rookie goon's underwear, which is pulled wedgie-style by the rest of the squad until it is ripped completely off. This is not an approved use-of-force technique. It is done on the bus between training exercises. It is best to not fight back.

Temporary goons do not usually have enough daily vinegar to make the squad. And their stuff might be unknown. At six foot one and 190 pounds, with a second-degree black belt in a two-thousand-year-old martial art and little interest in wrestling an HIV-positive agitator, I was officially the temporary-goon type in the estimation of the jail. I told no one that mattered about the two-thousand-year-old martial art. But I would like to say that I was the big-goon type: capable, but unwilling.

I watched the goon squad storm a cell once. That was as close as I got.

A fully uniformed goon squad is a riot. They wear black helmets, armor, gas masks, and anonymity. They blacken the hallway. I could not tell who it was that was marching in step and demonstrating the coming use of force by clicking on the shield. Even when one of them said to me, "S'up, Langston."

S'up, . . . man.

Negotiation to termination took six minutes. The pepper spray burned. The tear gas choked. The shield clicked on. The goons bulldozed. The agitator's feet went up. His body went down. He was rolled to his chest in a fast eight-armed flip. He was cuffed and shackled and spit-hooded. The shield clicked off.

It was Kill the Man—the kids' game—redux. Instead of catching the football and running from the mob of kids trying to tackle him, the agitator caught an attitude and tried to fight armored police. There is no winner in either the playground or the jail version. The Man is still the brave one, though. Or he is still the stupid one.

Either way, it is a voluntary role to play.

A big goon is not always large. He can be a five-foot-two former high school state champion wrestler with nothing else to prove. It does not matter if he is reluctant. Reluctant stuff makes an agitator who is agitating over four ounces of peanut butter comply the same as eager stuff—except with a big goon, there will be less scarring. Agitators should be thankful for that.

A little goon is not always small. He can be 265 pounds of steroids and wield the shield like a fucking F5 tornado. This is the worst kind of goon.

Incidentally, the reason why a two-thousand-year-old martial art still exists is because there have always been and always will be little goons. These little goons can take the shape of a realtor or a shipping manager or a racquetball-playing grandfather who cannot accept his advanced age because once when he was younger and did not have to pay for his hard-on, he had what he thought was an important job as a dean of some damn department in some damn college in some damn town on some damn planet like Earth.

Put two men alone on a metro train in Paris at night and study them. Sometimes they will size each other up. They will. And if it is not obvious who is dominant, they will grow a bulbous, rigid hate-on for each other.

This is the call of the goon.

I did not feel bad for the agitator who lost on the day that I watched the squad show their vinegar and stuff. When I had a shit week, and there was a certain agitator standing in front of me not complying, no matter how small the infraction—he might have just thrown his cigarette butt on the ground—I would have liked to kill the man.

I have some little goon in me on certain days.

All men do.

Any man can be a temporary goon.

So this goon types about goons.

Chumpy Joint Johns

THE Salisbury steak sent them hustling from cell to cell on BA block. Inmates stood at cell doors with arms full of chips, gingersnaps, packs of tuna,
bottles of hot sauce, any commissary they had.

At the closest cell, the outside inmate said, "That chumpy for three of
these johns."

The inside inmate said, "Make it four of them johns."

The chumpy was a bottle of jalapeño squeeze cheese. The johns were
beef and cheese sticks.

The outside inmate stood there considering it.

I'd take that trade. I have a thing for jalapeños.

They made the exchange.

Officially, trading commissary was prohibited. But I never once saw a
guard enforce that rule.

Two cells down I heard, "This chumpy for that joint."

The chumpy was a bacon single—actual precooked bacon, vacuum-
packed in plastic. The other, a box of vanilla wafers.

I thought that was a rip-off. But he took the trade. Bacon had power.

Five cells down, "Four Kite for one of them johns."

The Kite was the dollar-a-pack tobacco. The johns were jars of peanut
butter. The one with the johns was going to make a strong profit. Such was
the power of the hated Salisbury steak. People would be hungry.

I rounded the corner.

"I'll give you two johns to let me hold that chumpy tonight."

I saw that the johns were Newports—not whole packs, just single cigarettes. I stood still. I could never be sure what the chumpy, joint, or john was until I saw it. Those words replaced any noun. Code so inmates could talk contraband around staff or keep other inmates out of their business. The inmate in the cell handed him the chumpy. It was a stinger. I stepped forward and confiscated the chumpy. He still paid his johns. He had to. He should have been watching for me.

He said, "Come on, CO."

Everybody was getting ready to cook. Only the truly hard ate the Salisbury steak straight up. I could tell Stinger Inmate was mad. But that was okay. We were in jail. Mad was expected.

I walked back to the desk. The sergeant said, "Make a deposit." He slid a box out from under his desk. Ten cords lay knotted inside.

Then the sergeant pointed behind me and said, "Hand me a chumpy."

He meant a Styrofoam coffee cup. I handed it to him.

"Now one of those johns."

He meant a rubber band from the desk.

An inmate walked by and said, "Is this a new joint?"

He meant a new magic trick.

The BA sergeant, a short guy and part of the ruling majority (had a goatee), practiced magic tricks and pranks on pretty much an hourly basis. Magician took the paper clip out of my stinger, bent it into a wide V, and stretched the rubber band between the ends. It looked like a slingshot. He dug through the stinger box, found another clip, and hooked it to the middle of the rubber band. Then wound it like a propeller and stuffed it all into a Styrofoam cup. He squeezed the sides of the cup.

Another inmate walked up and asked, "What's the word, Sarge?"

Magician said, "I'm all coffeed out. Want a cup?"

The inmate said, "You know it. Thanks!"

Magician handed it to him and the paper clip inside spun and rattled like a rattlesnake.

The inmate said, "Damn!" and dropped the cup. When I saw the inmate laugh, I laughed too.

The phone rang. Magician didn't say a word and put it back down.

It was the All Call.

Magician rang the bell and into the PA announced, "Halftime in yard. Halftime. Go to yard."

Inmates stepped from their cells.

Melvin sprinted out the door.

I hadn't seen him in a month. Last time was on suicide watch, where he made a snow angel on the floor of his concrete container—for two hours straight. The snow: a torn-up magazine. The angel: he kicked and kicked. Grace moved him to the BA so he could be watched more closely. Maybe 120 guys lived there.

A chubby inmate walked onto the block carrying an electronic keyboard. Magician said, "You get your music on?"

He said, "I be making motherfuckers cry out there." Then rapped, "Them walls. Them walls. Them walls. Them walls be breaking our balls."

Magician said, "I see why they cried."

Then Magician said, "Who should I get next?" He reloaded the cup.

I went for a round.

An inmate named Hart stopped me at his cell. He had male pattern baldness, but hair down to the middle of his back. The jail allowed only two groups to have long hair: Rastafarians and Native Americans. Hart claimed to be Native American. I don't know what tribe. He had been talking to me for months, finding me in the yard and out on the walks. He used to be a trucker and told me, "You can order prostitutes over the radio. Lot lizards we call them. The best ones have no teeth."

Oh, I said.

He also told me that he was an expert at furniture reupholstering and that he basically ran the jail's furniture shop until "creative differences" with his boss.

His celly ignored me. Fresh from the academy I had stopped his celly for a pat search while on compound patrol. He said, "I bet you're one of those cops who took the job just to touch men."

An aggravator was what he was.

And that was on a day when I had six aggravators already. I told him, Yep, the stuff of dreams. He was bony and smelled like cigarettes. His uniform had faded from brown to pink. He was probably doing twenty years on a rape or murder charge. I patted a little rougher than I usually did.

He said, "You mad? Guards aren't allowed to get mad. Didn't they explain that to you in cop school?"

But that was almost a year earlier. There, on BA, Hart said, "Ignore my friend ignoring you. This foot locker shows more emotion than he does. He's hard."

Hart's friend didn't look up.

Magician called me over the PA to return to the desk.

Stinger Inmate followed me. He said, "Don't be nervous."

When we got to the desk, Magician handed Stinger Inmate the cup. He dropped it with a "Shit!" Then said to Magician, "Yo, I don't play." He didn't laugh. So I didn't laugh. Then he pointed to the stinger box and said, "Hey, let me get that john back."

Magician ignored him and said, "Who's next?"

Stinger Inmate walked away mad.

Magician turned to me and said, "Report to the dining hall to work the meal line. Then go eat."

So I reported to the dining hall.

The blocks rotated through. I sat inmates. They got mad at their seats. I kicked one out for trying to get a second tray. He got mad. I told another to take off his hat. He got mad. Another asked me, "Would you eat this?" It looked something like a turtle shell. He dumped it in the trash and walked out mad.

The Salisbury steak had that kind of effect.

BA block came in. Melvin was first and ate so fast that he maybe chewed twice. It made me sick to watch. He was gaining weight and went to begging food from the guys around him. They all gave him their steaks.

The angel ate and ate.

Hart got his food, sat at the next table, and stared at it. I told him to pace himself as a joke.

"It's shit," he said.

Then he said, "Call me a lieutenant. I want to complain."

I was pretty sure he wouldn't have said anything if I hadn't first, so I told him no. The lieutenant in charge of the meal that day was a hard-ass anyway. I wanted to save Hart the embarrassment.

Hart's friend walked into the dining hall. They looked at each other.

Hart stood and said, "I have the right to speak to a lieutenant. And it's your job to radio one."

I said no again, because, in fact, calling a lieutenant on the radio for inmate food complaints was not a mandatory part of my job.

He grit on me and yelled, "I've lost all respect for you!" He yelled it twice. Then flipped his hair and walked out of the dining hall. Not one inmate looked up because nothing new happened there.

It was jail.

The Salisbury steaks stank.

Men got mad.

~

THREE weeks later the Salisbury steak sent them hustling again from cell to cell on BA block. An inmate stood, arms full, at almost every cell door as I rounded the block.

"This joint for those johns."

The joint, a box of Frosted Flakes. The johns, a four-pack of vanilla pudding.

Around the corner I heard, "I need that chumpy tonight. I'll get you back Friday."

The chumpy, a box of instant rice. Friday was makeup day at the commissary.

The answer: "Hell nah."

Hart walked past me and avoided eye contact. He had been snubbing me since that day in the dining hall. I almost didn't recognize him. He had shaved his head. The first question he ever asked me was, "Are you a dick-head or a human?"

He must have decided.

Back at the desk, Magician told me that Hart was always emotional. "He's from a proud people." He laughed, then said, "His celly was hard, though. Never cried about nothing."

The phone rang. The bell rang. Inmates appeared.

Magician said, "Hand me that chumpy."

He meant the quarter he had just dropped. He rolled it along his knuckles. I left before he could make it appear from orifices.

I walked past Hart's cell. He sat at his desk.

Hart's friend's bunk was empty because he had just died.

A week earlier, Hart's friend was in the infirmary. And I was with his family on escort duty.

Hart's friend had noticed a painful lump on his left side, and the jail sent him out to the hospital for tests. The lump was pancreatic cancer, and once the hospital took a little piece to study, the tumor exploded. It quadrupled in size in a few days. He refused any further treatment. By the time I saw him again, his side was swollen and distorted from rib cage to hip. He was back in jail because it was cheaper to die there. The jail called his family. Two sisters and a brother showed up. They looked much younger. They followed me through the suicide-watch area.

Inmates lay in the fetal position in bunks back there. No sheets. No blankets. Lights on twenty-four hours a day.

In their brother's windowless room, I took a seat in the corner. Apparently I was there for security.

Hart's friend breathed slowly with long unnatural pauses between each breath. His family bent over him whispering until one of those pauses, then they would stop, look, listen, and wouldn't start talking until he breathed again. One of the sisters said to me, "You can leave." I looked at my boots. I didn't answer. She said it again, "You can leave. You can leave."

I told her I couldn't.

After an hour, Hart's friend started to come out of whatever sick foggy place he was dreaming of and said, "Fourteen Kite. I'll give you fourteen Kite." His voice was high-pitched and scratchy. His family looked at each other, not understanding. I didn't explain. It felt wrong to talk to his family. But I wondered what he wanted to buy. Fourteen Kite bought a lot of jail bacon.

The nurse came in, checked his slow vitals, and asked him if he was in pain and if he wanted another shot. The family said no. But Hart's friend said, "Yesh," so the nurse shot his IV and left.

Later the nurse told me how morphine slows respiration and circulation, how it speeds up the dying process. I sat with the family two hours watching the dying speed up. He didn't wake again while they watched. His family seemed to be waiting for something, some kind of insight, or redemption, or closure, I don't know, something profound maybe. But it was fourteen Kite. He'd give them fourteen Kite. That was the offer. That night he died.

~

I TAPPED on Hart's bars. He didn't look up. He rubbed his head. I tapped again. No response.

Back at BA's desk, a group of inmates gathered around Magician. He held the quarter and pulled back his sleeves. He yelled down the range to me, "Report to the dining hall. Then go eat."

So I reported.

The blocks rotated through. I sat inmates. They got mad at their seats. I kicked one out for pocketing the steak two feet in front of me. That was disrespectful. I got mad. He got mad. I told another to pull up his pants. He got mad. Another said, "Six bacon slices and squeeze cheese won't save this." He dumped it in the trash and walked out mad.

BA walked in. Melvin first again. He gasped for air between bites. The guys at his table laughed at how fast he cleared his tray. They probably didn't know his foster parents starved him.

Hart was last in line. He didn't look at me. He ate his Salisbury steak. He walked out and joined the rest of the inmates heading back to the blocks for count. One inmate patted him on the back.

Back on the block, I asked Magician about Hart's hair.

He said, "Native Americans shave it off when mourning."

I picked up my clipboard for count.

An inmate down the range screamed, "Suck a dick!" and kicked a table. It was Melvin.

Him kicking the table meant he was mad for losing the card game.

But, really, more like embarrassed. I couldn't be sure.

Magician looked at him for a second, blinked, and said, "He's running out of blocks to get kicked out of. Angry little demonic munchkin." Then he went back to work folding a paper into some kind of number trick. Two other guards stood watching the folding. They didn't seem affected by Melvin's outburst either.

The inmate playing with Melvin threw the deck of cards against the wall over Melvin's head and yelled, "Go and get them, bitch!"

That meant that he, too, was mad.

But, really, more like proud because it looked like he won. I couldn't be sure.

Melvin cowered and looked up at me.

I waved him toward me. But he turned and went to his cell.

Hart walked up to the desk and asked for a cell-change form. He had to bring in a new celly. Magician handed him the form. Then, once Hart left, said, "I'm watching that one. Close."

The other guards looked at Hart, that emotional man.

Openly sad men made the jail nervous. Cry and you got locked up. I saw weepy inmate after weepy inmate spend a week on suicide watch until the antidepressants took hold. That meant no job, no visits, no phone calls, and no privacy, even while shitting.

Punishment for those tears.

But anger was okay. Anger was a daily built-in experience. Anger was a lump in the Salisbury steak. It made you hard. Normal.

Inmates had good reason to be mad. They were in jail.

But guards weren't even allowed that.

We could leave.

An inmate walked into the middle of the block and said, "Why can't I find a taker for these johns?"

The johns were Honey Buns. He wanted two soups.

He looked angry.

But, really, he was probably sad. I couldn't be sure. It's hard to tell with men.

He said, "I'll throw in this joint."

The joint was a newspaper.

He sounded angry.

But, really, he was probably desperate and hungry. I still couldn't be sure. It's hard to tell. We've been trained.

Hart walked slowly with his cell-change form. He didn't look up. He rubbed his eyes, stepped into his cell, and pulled shut the door.

One of the other guards, a newer guy, said, "Look. He's crying. Real goddamn tears."

~

YOU become a guard and—poof—no more emotions. Not allowed.

So where do they go then, the emotions?

I FELT a lump.

House of Stain

ADMINISTRATIVE Custody, the AC, was hot and yellow and had twenty cells and a strip-search cage with a video camera and inmates living in limbo who stripped in that cage for that camera, then sat in their cells and waited. And waited. And sometimes it was months that they waited.

The AC was barricaded off from D block with sheet metal and roofed with what looked like an overgrown sewer grate. Very little natural light made it in. And D block's inmates, up on the higher ranges, dumped dirty sheets and crumpled passes and toilet-paper empties onto the grate because I-have-no-clue-why.

And on a night when I sat at the AC desk watching the garbage come down like rain—candy wrappers and fingernails and such, pitter-pattering—a parole violator turned himself in to the jail. His mother dropped him off. The control center cuffed him and brought him to me. We rarely had people come in straight from the street. It was strange to strip a guy out of civilian clothes.

But from within the strip cage within the AC cage within the D block cage, on camera, he handed me his shirt.

I said, Now your drawers.

He said, "Yes, sir."

He had designer glasses, new boots, a fresh haircut, and a foreskin that concealed no contraband.

I handed him his new outfit: boxers, T-shirt, and heelless jail slippers. All yellow. They were dyed like that so there would be no mix-ups in laundry. But the tinting was uneven, so the shirts and things came out looking urine-stained.

A lieutenant with a white beard stood behind me during the search. He said, "Welcome back!"

Then looking right and proper for jail, dripping in wrinkled yellow, Polite Violator said, "Thank you, sir."

I showed him to his cell. He stepped in and hit the button on the light fixture like he had been living there a year.

Meanwhile, it was my first week of post-trainee freedom. I had survived one year at the jail, conforming, enough, to become a full-on corrections officer. And I was to marry in three weeks. The wedding in Iowa. The arboretum reserved. The harp player booked.

Back at the desk, my partner, the ex-landscaper who welcomed Melvin to Rockview, told me, "That wedding ring will pull your finger right off. Almost lost mine jumping off a truck. Got hung up on the tailgate. Dislocated my finger and everything."

The ripped-up wrapper of a soup pack fell through the roof grate. Inmate confetti.

I yelled up, Knock it off, asshole!

I could say things like that then. I was trying on different insults. At a year in, you are hard to fire. A perk of having a union.

"I've got your asshole, yo," the transgressor yelled down.

Twice as many confetti scraps floated down. Followed by the empty seasoning packets.

~

AFTER you make it a year, if liked, you go into a block or, even better, the control center. But this is by invitation only. If not liked, you spend your days in the yard or filling in for block guards on their days off. Or worse, you fill in for the trainees in the trainee jobs.

Imagine working the showers for twenty-five years.

What I wanted was a block for my own. A big one. Full-time block officers got to run the blocks. Make the announcements. Control the flow. Do something other than turning a damn key.

I attached myself to the D block crew. After a day in the yard or AC or wherever, I hung out in D after final count. I subbed in the card games for whichever block officer was off. I showed well at hearts. Most blocks played spades, but hearts was my game. After a month, Shrek asked, "Do you want to join the crew?"

I said, I do.

That was an important moment. A couple weeks off training status and already initiated into one of the biggest blocks in the jail would mean respect and status and prove that I was a man among men.

But the next day Shrek told me, "Sometimes my pecker tingles when my leg falls asleep. And Captain Grace said you can't join the crew. He gave no reason." Which induced suspicion in the D crew, and paranoia in me.

Which made that my last card game.

And I went home that night to a silent treatment from my fiancée. I wasn't sure how to handle it. Things had been going well. We went for runs together. We found a great deal on a Mexican resort for the honeymoon. I was ready for the nuptials despite Landscaper saying things like, "Enjoy the honeymoon. Then the divorce."

But she was interesting and smart. Driven in ways I would never be. I saw a successful future.

~

AT roll call the day after the D block rejection, Grace told me, "Sunscreen, Langston. You'll need it today. And hydrate."

I had yard. It was June.

I said, 10–4, sir. And headed out and watched the inmate softball game. Two foul balls in a row came at me.

Not suspicious at all.

I walked with a lifetime yard officer. He stepped to a seventy-year-old inmate and said, "You think you're fucking tough?," then to the next old-head he came across, "What about you? You tough?" and to the next, who used a walker, "I know you ain't tough, son. Lord knows you ain't. And hurry up, would you? I'm trying to walk here."

He kept looking at me for a laugh. I told him we better split up before a lieutenant saw us. Rule was we had to walk separate.

Thankfully.

I found a sliver of shade by the fence.

Block-banned officers were defective. And the jail banished them.

Bully elderly inmates? Enjoy the yard, yo.

Forever.

Then I dodged foul balls the next three days. The touch football games were the worst. Someone always wanted to fight over being tagged too hard. And the ice cream shack was open. Inmates needed ice cream tickets to buy Dilly Bars and ice cream sandwiches. So they panhandled and begged from each other nonstop. And wanted to gamble. And fight. And yell. And Melvin sat on the bleachers surrounded by wrappers. Then sat drawing in the dirt. Then bobbed from group to group dancing for tickets.

~

I RAN by myself at home. My fiancée didn't seem interested. I knew this because she still wasn't talking.

And here I had mastered not telling her about foreskins. I didn't tell her that I basically breathed Salisbury steak farts on certain days. I didn't want to disturb her with jail and its minutiae. Like the festering belly-button wound my wrist bumped while handing out toilet paper in the infirmary. I didn't mention to her how the nurse told me that it was flesh-eating bacteria, one of those bugs that's antibiotic resistant. I said nothing about the nurse saying, "Here, fast, use this sanitizer. Rub it on right away. Right away!"

I said, Damn.

Jail speak for Did my life just end?

Didn't my fiancée appreciate my lack of engagement? And to answer her question about the townhouse: "Doesn't it suck how the floors creak here?"

Sure, of course.

Totally sucks.

Even when, actually, there was no "Sure, of course." No register, really, at all. Just a flat gaping indifference of I didn't care. Didn't she know I carried dead people one minute, then walked through our front door the next?

Ah, right, never told her that.

But it was an effective way, I thought, of managing the span from gate and mate.

~

GRACE had me in the AC the next week, so I handed out meals and mail and turns in the shower for the yellow and Polite Parole Violator. "Thank you, sir."

He was a fixture. He stood at his cell bars a day later and thanked me for the flex pen—a bendy ballpoint pen that cannot be made into a weapon or instrument of suicide. His haircut was no longer fresh. He thanked me for the state toothpaste a day later, clean splattered boxers a few later after that, and on the next, for kicking away a burning wad of toilet paper dropped outside his cell from above. He wore a do-rag that time. A piece of sheet.

He waited for his file to be located and reviewed and would not be allowed in general population until his drug history, violent tendencies, and escape proclivities were analyzed by qualified state professionals.

Polite Violator could go straight to the special needs block if he was schizo, or to BB if he was down for touching kids. But, most likely, he would make it for one of the door-slamming big blocks that I coveted.

He asked, "Am I being punished, sir?"

I told him I wished I knew.

My fiancée: still silent.

Want isolation? Work on a crowded acre of grass, hundreds strong, watching Melvin bob around, then go home to a dark house.

But we went to a tanning salon together so we would look healthy and happy for the wedding. She corrected her students' papers. She worked her grad courses.

I didn't tell her about my own corrections, my lack of place at the jail, my sudden self-doubt.

Somehow, this was supposed to help.

You're welcome, honey.

~

I SHOOK open a trash bag and collected Polite Violator's Styrofoam dinner plates, then stepped down to the chronic complainer in the next cell.

The complainer was skinny, with lopsided dreadlocks. His cell covered in papers. "I'm in the DOC's head," he said and handed me his trash with two grievances.

"More trash," Landscaper said when I threw the grievances in the mail pile. He said, "This is why we have landfill problems."

I thought about directly asking Grace what I did wrong. Go too long without a block and you are forsaken. An untouchable. Clearly damaged.

Landscaper asked, "What's with that polite inmate anyway? What's he hiding?"

Guards expected the worst. Always.

The inmates around Polite Violator were already figured out. General population didn't work for them.

Sodomize a celly? Enjoy the twice-a-week shower.

Send love notes to your counselor? Enjoy the no tobacco.

Win a fight? Enjoy the strip cage.

Lose a fight? Enjoy the stains. No one said jail was fair.

Most stays in the AC were short. A temporary dump into a cell until the inmate's misconduct hearing found him guilty, sentencing him to an extended visit in the bucket.

I traded Polite Violator some clean yellow drawers for some dirty yellow drawers.

I apologized to my fiancée. Still nothing. Landscaper said, "Trade her in."

He said, "Time for a new model."

Some existed in the AC for longer bids until they were yellow and pale, like a police-academy-dropout-turned-thief who waited on the results of a drug test because he had bloodshot eyes and called Grace "bro" two months earlier.

He took up fishing with a cord braided from blanket strings. He cast the line out with trade offers: maybe a ketchup packet for some Sweet'N Low. If the guy two or five cells down agreed, he netted it with his sheet and tied his trade on. Drug Test would then reel his line back in.

While delivering mail I rounded the corner and stomped on his line. Just reacted. Drug Test had yanked it so fast I thought it was a roach.

He said, "Damn, CO, it's just jelly."

It was grape, and I took it, string and all. The range was the guards' turf.

While I gathered up the line, dust bunnies came down through the grate. It was that minute's weather pattern. There could be haircut dustings, orange-peel drizzle, apple-core hail, or cigarette-butt meteor showers, which looked cool at night.

I delivered the rest of the mail. Polite Violator was polite. The chronic complainer complained. He received a letter from a congressman. He said, "Cruel and unusual" when I stuck it in the bars.

He had been in the AC for four months then, bitching all the while.

The Department of Corrections recognized him as a chronic pain in its big blocky ass. Sometimes institutions traded problem inmates to give their officers a break from them. The chronic complainer had no file either. His last institution had "lost" it.

Bitching gets you nowhere in jail.

I decided to not ask Grace about D block.

I told the complainer that at least he had time to think.

"Yeah," he said. "But I'm thinking about all the wrong things."

Such as?

"The wrong things, CO. Can I get a razor?"

I told him to talk to morning shift about that.

Something that looked like peach yogurt landed close by. It smelled like feet.

"You're lucky, asshole!" the yogurt bomber yelled.

"Here's what you can do for that," Landscaper yelled up. "Seek anger management. And fuck off. And, matter of fact, I'm coming up now."

The sounds of a man running in jail slippers faded away.

A call came across the radio. "AC, meet me at the gate."

White Beard lieutenant brought in Melvin.

Melvin bragged, "One and down! One shot and he went down!" I stripped him in the camera cage. His left shoulder was scraped up. He had started and lost a fight and was looking at another ninety days of bucket time but felt right and fine that moment.

I handed him his yellow. But Melvin, I said. There goes your summer.

The bars clinked.

He said, "Life is shit."

~

NEXT shift I left the roll-call room with the parade of yard officers. I stood far from the softball field. I had picked up my wedding band that morning. It fit a little loose.

A pigeon shit on the bill of my hat. I took it off and wiped it on the grass.

Polite Violator walked by on the gravel loop with two guys from D block. He nodded at me. He looked strange wearing brown. I was jealous.

My fiancée had told me my transgression before shift. She said, "Last time we ran together, you told me I ran too slow."

A silent treatment for a comment. I couldn't relate. I could call a guard an anal secretion and wouldn't have to apologize. Even if I meant it. This would probably even increase my popularity.

But it wasn't in jail. And I had told her she ran too slow with an exasperated tone. Like, hurry up, would you? Like, why ain't you tough? Like, seriously, why ain't you? Yard officer speak.

I was sorry, I said.

But seek anger management on that, is what I meant.

And life is shit. Didn't she know?

I applied my jail relationship strategies.

Took a year to learn.

Would take ten to unlearn.

I nodded back to the violator and thought all the wrong things.

Alternating Currents

THE Pennsylvania electric chair looks like a picnic table put together wrong. It's five feet tall, made of oak, each board thick and lacquered. Eight straps restrained the condemned. Brackets and bolts and straps and a headrest, that's the chair. And 350 people were electrocuted while resting their heads against it.

THE chair was gone, taken by the Pennsylvania Museum Commission and not put on display when I walked into the death room. The room: painted white and trimmed in oak. The windows: still barred. I knew it as the training room. In it, guards refreshed guards on how to guard. Since I had a year in, I had to go through the classes again.

THE chair's official nickname was "Old Smokey." But guards called it "The Space Maker" and "Payback" and "The Amazing Electric Garbage Disposal."

I SAT on a folding chair at a folding table listening to a guard read about cell and area searches. To get there, I climbed the spiral stairs in the death house, nicely named the Deputy Warden Building, at the center of the jail. There's an elevator, but I never saw it used—not even by the training lieutenant with the false teeth whose office used to be the morgue. The refreshing guard asked rhetorical questions like, "Is it professional to sniff inmate underwear while searching?"

Giggles all around.

IN 1834, Pennsylvania became the first state in the country to stop public executions. All hangings after then were private and individually run by the counties. But then Smokey took over. That was 1915, and it was considered more humane. The death house was the first building completed on the compound. Before inmates even lived in the main cellblock, an electrocution took place.

> The inaugural, John Talap, who had murdered his wife, was "badly frightened" when he walked into the room before being "quickly settled into the chair and strapped in." Smokey put him to rest in four minutes.

Pennsylvania dismantled Smokey in 1972 when it ruled the death penalty unconstitutional. Then PA reassembled Smokey in 1985 when it declared death constitutional again. The constitution hadn't changed. Then it took Smokey apart again in 1990 when it deemed electrocution inhumane. Lethal injection took over. And that's when the room turned to training. Today, injections happen down at the new execution house, a building separate from the main compound. It has its own fence, its own motion sensors, its own flowers. It used to be a sanitarium. It has just three cells. Rockview never had a death row. Inmates get shipped in, housed for one night, fed, then dead.

> Paul Jaworski led the "Flatheads" gang based out of Detroit in the 1920s. The newspapers called him a "Bandit Chief." His gang perpetrated America's first armored car robbery. They used a land mine for the job, buried it under a road, and made off with $104,000. Execution witnesses said that he looked dazed and had to be supported by two guards on his way to the chair on account of his dead leg—it was paralyzed in the shootout with the cops. The doctor declared the rest of him dead at 7:06 a.m., January 21, 1929.

The "use of force" class reminded me that "force" is any action by a staff member intended to compel an inmate to act or to cease acting. The "use of force continuum" is a guard's guideline to all those compelling actions. Here is the continuum:

1. Show of force (standing outside an inmate's cell is a show of force).

2. Control techniques (verbal commands / handcuffs / shackles), oleoresin capsicum (pepper spray), electronic body immobilizing device (stun gun).

3. Chemical munitions (tear gas).

4. Active countermeasures (strikes against the inmate) and/or specialty impact munitions (beanbag rounds).

5. Firearms.

The instructor said, "Force is not authorized as a means of punishment or revenge. So, here's a question: If you're disrespected by an inmate, can you handcuff him by his skinny fucking ankles high up on the bars of his cell door?"

Much laughter.

NOTHING separated the spectators from the condemned. No wall, no door, no safety-glass window, just hoods. One hood on the prisoner's head, the other an exhaust hood above the chair. The witnesses sat on benches with no backs. At the end of each sat brass spittoon–looking puke buckets. The burnt flesh and hair smell lasted ten or fifteen minutes. Executions required a minimum of six witnesses, six newspeople, and up to four victims of each condemned. From every account I've read, victims sat "impassively." No tears, no cheers reported by the papers. At Ted Bundy's execution in Florida, the witnesses didn't celebrate, but outside, a crowd of five hundred, who didn't see the electrocution, did.

> Floyd Smith tried to abandon an infant at night but said he "got scared when a dog barked" and said he fell on the baby. The baby died by crushing. He put the body in a creek because he was afraid of being charged with murder . . . then he was later charged with murder. On March 6, 1923, he was pronounced dead at 7:17 a.m. All electrocutions took place in the morning so Rockview wouldn't have to disrupt its routine. The guards on the execution team probably helped with the breakfast line afterward. The most popular breakfast at Rockview was anything with bacon. You could smell it cooking from inside the training room.

I HELD the stun gun to my thigh for twenty seconds. The room filled with ozone. You weren't a man if you couldn't go all twenty. The gun shut off automatically at twenty. The prongs left little burn marks, even through clothes. To survive the class, you had to make sure no one walked up behind you. A stun to the neck is a special sensation.

TEN years before I took the guard job and climbed the spiral staircase, I drove by Rockview and saw picketers across the street protesting an execution. The sign held by one of them, a man in a red coat, read, "Murder By State Is Still Murder."

AFTER an inmate stabbed to death another inmate in 1991, the spokesman for Rockview at the time said, "To my knowledge, it's the first murder in the prison."

On July 30, 1928, Joseph Kamenisky, twenty years old, became the 184th man to rest his head on Smokey. That was thirteen years after the first. He confessed to shooting his physician. The physician had amputated of one of Kamenisky's legs after a mine accident. Using crutches, he "unfalteringly" made his way from the cell to the death chamber. Not once did an inmate physically resist walking to Smokey.

"Use of restraints" is the nice way to say handcuffs and shackles and spit shields and waist chains and black boxes and heavy leather Melvin-restraining straps. A black box is the plastic box that clamps over the handcuff chain and keyholes. It connects the cuffs to the waist chain. I stood cuffed and shackled, waisted and boxed—couldn't move my hands more than six inches. Pain was my partner stepping on the shackle chain, which pulled those large cuffs down on my heels. Use of restraint was me not doing it to him on his turn. The instructor said, "Here's the unbreakable rule: once the cuffs are on, you can't hit them. That's a punk move. You know, wrong. So don't be in a rush to cuff them."

ROBERT Elliott became Pennsylvania's official executioner in 1926 when his predecessor committed suicide. Elliott worked for five different states at the same time and was paid $150 for each of his almost four hundred executions, the most of any official American executioner. Near the end of his career, Elliott said that he felt he was "an arm of organized society, carrying out its will just as a jury convicts and a judge sentences." He traveled with a kit: the leather cap, the sponges, the trained hands that adjusted straps. He never looked at the condemned's face, fixing the cap and hood from behind.

> In 1931, Irene Schroeder, the "Blonde Bandit," became the first woman electrocuted in Pennsylvania. On Smokey she wore a gray dress and no outward sign of emotion. Robert Elliott said that of all the executions, hers haunted him the most.

Even though it's listed in my employee handbook, I never had this class: "Stress Management." Sorry, fiancée. And there was no class on positive coping mechanisms either. Sorry, liver. Luckily, though, I passed the riot baton class. Really crushed it.

SMOKEY wasn't electrified. Smokey restrained. One electrode carried the current from the control panel on the wall to the leather cap. The electricity made the plunge through a saltwater-soaked sponge and a shaved spot on top of the head. The other electrode carried the current back—it was strapped low on one leg to complete the circuit—that way, the whole body could share in the damage. The pants leg was split in advance. The "electrician" administered three shocks. The first, 2,000 volts (wall sockets are 120), lasted for twenty seconds. The volts are unimportant, though—it's the amperes, or amps, the rate of those volts through the body, that does the damage. Two thousand volts with a complete circuit on Smokey produced 7 to 12 amps (0.07 amps for three seconds is considered a fatal amount). Everyone's a little more or less electrically resistant. To electricity, people are just walking, sloshing, person-shaped conductors. The first shock knocked out the condemned and stopped the heart. The second shock, at 250 volts and 2 to 5 amps, went for a minute to keep the heart from starting again, for what's called heart death. The third shock was the same as the first, the triple tap, just in case. Common physical reactions to the current were bloody sweat, bloody drool, bright red skin, gurgles, and evacuation of bowels. By the end, the body was close to 140 degrees—beef cooked rare, according to the meat thermometer in my kitchen.

> In 1932, while Joseph Kosh was waiting to be executed, he tried to kill himself by hanging (sheet), stabbing (pencil), and burning (sheet, newspaper, magazine, toilet paper, and matches). Then he was electrocuted.

All of the above. That's the answer to at least a third of the questions on a Pennsylvania Department of Corrections test. Here's a sample question on "Hostage Survival":

1) Choose the best answer. When taken as a hostage you should:
   A. Keep your cool
   B. Appear human
   C. Take note of everything you see and hear
   D. Resist rape
   E. All of the above

The answer's E. But B is the one I think about the most. Does the uniform make a person appear inhuman? Does that mean jail is inhumane?

> Alexander Meyer, the "lust killer," admitted to chasing down a sixteen-year-old girl with his truck, raping and murdering her, then throwing her body down a well. He complained that the cell in the death house didn't have a radio. On July 12, 1937, Smokey's room sounded like an electric bass guitar when Meyer completed the circuit. It hummed medium pitch for the 2,000-volt hit, deeper for the 250, then back up for the finale. The only other noise came from Meyer himself, straining the restraints: leather creaking, buckles clinking.

For CPR class, we had a bucket of mouths for the armless, legless rescue dummies. I took a mouth, kneeled down, and inserted it. I checked for responsiveness, opened the airway using the head-tilt chin-lift method, and initiated rescue breaths. The instructor said, "No tongues! Why are you tonguing him? Stop tonguing him!" He said, "Just kidding. But hey, just make it look good." The next guard stepped up and used a flying elbow drop to check for responsiveness, hammer fists to open the airway, and for rescue breaths, pile drivers. The instructor said, "Nice chest compressions. Next."

THIS is when deadly force is authorized by the Pennsylvania DOC:

   1. To prevent serious bodily harm to self or others.
   2. To protect property from damage or destruction only if such damage or destruction could reasonably cause serious bodily harm to self or others.
   3. To prevent escape from a correctional facility while in immediate pursuit.
   4. For the recapture of an escapee.

Executions aren't on the list.

In 1962, Elmo Smith ate potatoes, lima beans, and peach shortcake. Three years earlier he had raped and beaten a seventeen-year-old girl, then dumped her in a ditch. He confessed that she was still alive and begging for her life. Above the girl's pubic area he drew an arc and fire with her lipstick. An expert witness identified the drawing as St. Elmo's fire. Elmo Smith was the last person—number 350—to die on Smokey. During his execution, one witness held his breath when "the smoke started to come out of [Elmo's] head." St. Elmo is the patron saint of sailors. His fire is considered a good omen—it appears when the worst of the storm is over.

Then the lethal injection building opened up in 1990. So Rockview lethally injected three. They volunteered. And a few die every year waiting for it. Then, in 2015, Pennsylvania banned capital punishment temporarily. The governor described the system as all of the above: flawed, endless, unjust, and ineffective.

MOST training didn't help. One day I gave Melvin a roll of toilet paper so he could wipe his tears. The next day I ticketed a guy for throwing a toilet-paper wad at me. Next day helped an elderly lifer off the ground in the yard. Next day raged at a young kid for baring his teeth at me. Next day shook the hand of a murderer for telling me I dropped my keys. Next day almost fought a car thief for giving me the finger. And every day I heard this from guards: "Forget the training. These are the rules of jail: no fighting, no fornicating. Everything else is gray."

~

SIXTY percent of Americans support the death penalty. To the cheering 60 percent I say this: imagine a guy in a full-body cuff. There are a thousand pounds of nickel-plated steel bands wrapped around this guy. A metal mummy. Each band a foot thick. You can't even really see him. But you know he's inside. If he wiggles too far, razor wire cuts him. Any farther and guns shoot him. So he doesn't wiggle much. He can't walk free. Can't buy what he wants or see his family when he wants or even shower or use a phone when he wants. But this guy is still alive. He's fed through a slot in one side. He kind of shifts around and contorts himself to take a drink. He makes use of his little space. Through small movements he sometimes creates art, like a handmade birthday card for his daughter with Minnie Mouse and everything. He somehow turns ordinary markers into airbrushes to do it. But sometimes he creates nothing in particular. Sometimes he just fiddles with a chip in the metal or plays cards or kind of does these mini squats to stay in shape. He keeps busy in his cuff. He has to. He's alive. But sometimes he'll bang an elbow or ankle and has to be put in a smaller cuff for a month until he learns to be safe again. His bigger cuff feels better then. But he can still only wiggle. He ages inside. He learns new trades and forgets old trades and gets used to the full-body cuff the best he can. Can you see him in there whistling or sharing food with another metal mummy, or maybe you catch him crying at night because that's it, that's all he gets, a full-body cuff? Good. Now imagine him being beaten to death with electricity or chemicals.

What kind of move is that?

Natural Manliness

HERE'S how to turn a man into a mustache: send him to jail. Pay people to identify him not as a father. Not as a son. Not as a contributor to the greater herd. But as "That guy in cell 113. The one with the stupid mustache. He's yours. He stinks."

Drill the paid people on this. This is for protection. Dehumanize that human. Avoid that hurt.

And I stripped the Pencil-Thin Mustache. Him in the cell. Me in the hallway. My commands delivered through the food slot like that morning's biscuits.

He flicked his tongue suggestively.

I suggested he take it seriously before I took it seriously. I said this so the lieutenant in charge would hear.

Pencil-Thin took it seriously.

And I cuffed the mustache through the slot. Then unlocked the mustache's door. Then told the mustache to stand at the wall.

The mustache obeyed.

And I stepped into the cell to search for contraband: from porn to weapons to an extra pair of underwear, I would have it all.

Then I would repeat the process twenty times for twenty non-fathers and non-sons.

I cuffed Caveman Bush. I put cuffs on Amish Neckbeard. I cuffed Red Mustache—his right arm in a full cast, so I ratcheted the other cuff to the bars at the end of the range.

He said, "This is stupid."

I said, Yes, this is kind of stupid.

Then stepped into his cell.

I cuffed Sparse Fuzz. I cuffed Whiskery 'Stache. I had bad news for those two. If they couldn't grow a decent scruff by twenty, they couldn't grow a decent scruff. Not even when scruff is trendy. Not even by shaving and shaving to thicken the hair—because that's a myth. It won't thicken. I've tried.

I cuffed Pointy Beard and Trimmed Mustache. I cuffed his celly, Gray Beard. His beard just as pointy. His mustache just as trimmed. Even his neck was clean. His beard brushed my wrist when he bent sideways to pull up his jumpsuit with his teeth. I yanked my hand back.

He flinched and said, "Sorry, youngin."

I said, It's okay, oldin.

I stepped in the cell and searched for their contraband razor. Well-trimmed facial hair had no place in the bucket on a Tuesday. They could only shave Wednesdays. It was the jail of the jail in there, a well-lit and climate-controlled storage locker where inmates measured time by beard length.

And I flipped and squeezed the mattresses, shook the sheets, inspected the light fixtures. In the sink: curly hairs. Were they chinnies? assies? I couldn't find the razor. They likely flushed it.

I cuffed Never-Ending Neckline next door. Before his bucket visit, he was chiseled and angled with razor-sculpted manliness. Chin art. But after sixty bucketed days for mouthing off to a guard with a shaggy goatee, his cheeks were fuzz. His sheets, the same: dusted with short-and-curlies. I shook them out and listened for contraband hitting the floor.

I cuffed the Fu Man Chu. I put cuffs on Muttonchops. I cuffed Lincoln Beard. I put cuffs on Natural Soul Patch. I cuffed Full Beard but Bald and got my cuffs caught in his wrist fur. "Fuck, son," he said. "You're pulling. You're pulling."

Stand at the wall, is all I said. You got no respect for being gentle in jail. Or apologetic. But it was surprising to hear him cry. I thought body hair was supposed to be manly. I thought arm, chest, and face hair came with ingrown pain tolerance and man knowledge, like knowing to put the beer can in the cozy before opening it (otherwise it's hard to put in—the can goes all soft and crinkly). If you're a man and didn't know that, well, you're not a man, according to a bearded bucket guard who said that man hair has been a natural force of human sexuality since way back, since squat-in-cave way back when men fought, women thought, and the hairiest chests won the most breasts.

Full Beard but Bald said, "What's that smell? That baby powder? You still in diapers?"

I said, It's freedom.

It was my lotion, probably. Full Beard but Bald didn't respond. I stepped in his cell and took his dismantled library book—it was something about the history of farming tools. There was a stack of paper with instructions on how to build gates, plow handles, and baby cradles from spare oak barrels. It looked like frontiersman stuff. Like it belonged to the men who cleared the land in Rockview's valley two centuries earlier to make way for the iron furnaces.

I took Full Beard's pieces of paper, his shreds of sheets, his towers of trash. Bucket shakedowns meant guards became garbagemen. I liked it. Less standing around. More purpose. The jail shook the bucket down randomly, once a quarter. Scheduled randomness.

Shakedowns let me practice with cuffs. You want the keyholes facing you. If the holes face the inmate, he has to contort his arms, or you have to bend in close to get at them. I wanted the cuffs tight but not loud—meaning, I didn't want to hear the inmate complain. And the less time I spent taking the cuffs off, the more time the inmate thought I had in. So I went fast.

I cuffed Three-Day Stubble—a fresh bucket recruit. I cuffed White Patch in a Brown Field. I cuffed Braided Chin.

I tried to fake like I had years in, talking tough: Hush, puppy. Pucker up, buttercup. Be sweet, baby. But my smooth, young face betrayed me always. No beard. Barely a shadow. And I had to own my newish face by treating it with lotion to protect it from the harsh climate of jail.

"You smell good," Braided Chin said.

I squeezed the cuffs extra tight.

I cuffed Handlebars. Those old-timey and manly curls didn't keep him from saying, "Damn that's cold!" I cuffed Nose Hair Mustache All in One. I put cuffs on Round Crooked Thing with crumbs. He pulled on them to check the tightness.

I told him to stand at the wall.

I didn't worry about anyone picking the cuffs. I never saw—or even heard of—an inmate picking any at the jail. But I saw guards practice. And I practiced.

You can pick cuffs with a paper clip. Simple as turning a barrel into a gravity-fed goat feeder:

- Straighten the clip. Flatten the end.
- Shove it in—but not in the keyhole—shove it in the jaw. The jaw's the part with the teeth.
- Squeeze the cuff tighter—yes tighter—that works the clip further into the cheek. The cheek's the part with the keyhole.
- While shoving the clip, pull back on the jaw.
- Marvel at your freedom.

This is called shimming. You can hide a shim in your beard or, if you have the time and the patience, in your colon.

Flat pieces of metal work best. A flattened battery's shell will do it. Or a bobby pin—just pull the plastic ball off the end first. Disposable razor blades too: remove them from the plastic, then dull them on concrete to save your fingers. Fashioning a perfect replica of a cuff key from a paper clip, in my experience, is pretty damn hard. Even with needle-nose pliers and an actual key for reference. But straightening out a clip, then hammering the end flat with a rock, this can be done in a minute.

When not on a shakedown, guards didn't carry cuff keys—keys risked the security of the institution. And so did guys like Blond Beard jerking around at the end of the hall during the shakedown. I had just stepped out of Full-on Santa Beard's cell with a bag of bads: a dozen plastic spoons melted into the female form, a towel crocheted from a torn-up sheet, and six orange husks. Each husk had a little hole. That's how he ate them. He told me, "Hate them sticky fingers."

And Blond Beard yelled, "Don't touch my mail!"

Mail was the one freedom bucket inmates received, but still searchable. Probably the best place to hide a razor blade.

And Lieutenant Four-Day Scruff told him, "Don't you do it. Don't you break my cuffs."

If shimless, you have to bend the hell out of cuffs to get them off. You won't be able to break the chain, so don't try. Instead, use the edge of a bunk, the lip of a jail table. Then pull. Then push. Figure out which. Eventually they'll bend far enough to pop open.

Oh, and this hurts. That bony lump on your wrist—the ulnar styloid process, it's called—gets torn up and bruised.

Blond Beard managed to bend Lieutenant Scruff's pair on the edge of the door, but not open them.

"You bought 'em," Scruff said. "You bought 'em."

Money for the cuffs would be taken out of the inmate's account.

Blond Beard walked into his cell, back up to the slot to be unlocked. It took Scruff five minutes to get them off. "Your fault," Scruff said as he twisted and pulled, maybe being dramatic.

I cuffed Gray Chinny.

I put cuffs on Patchy Melvin. Still in there for his version of brawling. If I didn't see him around the jail, I knew he was in the bucket yelling about how his last name was a lie. I told him to walk to the door. He said, "You. I know you. You didn't get enough of my cock last time?"

He yelled at Lieutenant Scruff, "Look! Look! I'm grown! I'm grown!" while pulling on his patchy beard.

He backed up to the slot so I could cuff him. Him turning his wrists didn't affect me that time.

"My cock!" he yelled. "Get off my cock!"

I started to not like him.

I said, Stand at the wall, Patches.

Steel is ninety-eight parts iron and at most two parts carbon. Go more than two parts carbon, it's considered cast iron. Antique cuffs are cast iron—heavy, clunky, primitive things. Like horseshoes with bolts.

I cuffed Jet-Black and Full. I put cuffs on Tight and Trimmed. I couldn't find his razor either. I confiscated a milk carton a month expired, meaning, I threw it away. Eight full trash bags sat at the end of the range.

Jails classify handcuffs as temporary restraining devices. But they've always been around. Nickel-plated now, sure, but still primitive: a device that temporarily binds.

I cuffed Boxed Beard. "Come on," he said. "Too tight. Too tight."

Boxed Beard said, "It took determination to grow this. You soft."

I cuffed Skunk Goatee.

Facial hair in jail was part of the endless fight for individuality among the uniformed many. I saw it in the military with tattoos, sunglasses, and sideburns. The majority of guards grew it. The majority of inmates too.

I tried to cuff Loud Beard. "My shoulder!" he yelled. "My shoulder! You gotta cuff me in front."

Lieutenant Scruff said, "Go ahead. Do it, so we don't hear him flap."

The problem was that he was so obese and so inflexible that he had trouble even dressing himself.

"Hey," Loud Beard said. "I'm a man."

He pulled on his beard to show me. Proof in the puff. It touched his chest. But his cheeks were trimmed. He had a razor, too. A good one, it looked.

I cuffed him in front, ratcheted them down the standard amount, with enough room for a pinky to fit.

"You's a kid," Loud Beard said. "A baby-faced kid." And he, all manly, scratched his cheek. It was an awkward two-hands-in-cuffs scratch.

I looked at him. That Loud Beard. That guy in cell 122. Not a father. Not a son.

He shimmied to the side. I stepped into his cell and picked up his mail.

On top: a card with a football, a barbell, and a "World's Best Dad" printed in faded blue ink.

And it cut me.

Hayyyyyyy

GRACE tried Melvin on CA once paroled from the bucket, but that wasn't the talking point in the roll-call room. The topic: how was CA going to run with a female sergeant, a female trainee, and me? Two females on one block! Imagine it. To make things worse, according to uniformed males, the roving officer for CA and CB was also a female. There would be a half hour when she would relieve me for chow, which would leave three women in charge of two hundred men. Some of those men in for rape and domestic abuse. All of them with penises.

Uniformed males pulled on my sleeve and whispered into my ear to "Watch your back" and "Make sure to have the radio close" and "Your sergeant is fighting above her weight," and they wouldn't stop with it.

So I walked on the block all tense. The sergeant: small, short hair, and known for once being knocked out by an inmate who outweighed her by 150 pounds. This left her with occasional migraines and reputation for being hard as flint. Most guards quit after an assault.

She told me, "Showers, open them up."

So I did. The block was only two ranges in the shape of an L, the showers directly under the bubble. The bubble in the elbow of the L.

Melvin came right up and said, "This is my house and you trespassin'."

The showers are your house?

"Why you always playing?"

You going to take a shower today?

"You'd like that, wouldn't you?"

We all would. Trust me.

"Man, fuck you."

It was the most coherent he had been in a month. Maybe CA was good for him.

Sergeant Flint yelled down, "Melvin! Come here. Now!"

"Oh," he said. "Mom is mad." And ran up the stairs.

She lectured him on language choices and how officers were here to keep him safe and that he could do it, stay safe, but he needed to watch his language with staff he didn't know because using inappropriate language with the wrong staff member could make him unsafe and did he understand?

"Yes, ma'am," he said. "But I've known him since forever."

"Okay," she said.

And that was why he was doing so well. Actual corrections.

Inmates entered and exited the showers in towels, and my whole sensory world became that wet industrial soap rank. I looked in every two minutes or so. Gave the room a quick scan. It kept full at fifteen. Inmates ran to yard and ran to school and ran to whatever helped run off the time.

Each block felt different. The dark and closed-in CA seemed relaxed. Blocks run by the hard-rolling crews produced a sort of unsettling quiet and constant stares from the inmates. On CA, though, inmates chatted and laughed. They had trust. Flint ran it like a professional. Clear expectations. No screaming. Minimal misconducts. Fairness.

Really, you could terrorize every inmate around you, insulting their mothers and such, and making it a personal goal to have the jail's two thousand furious with you and survive just fine. As long as you did it equally.

But be unfair when it came time to hand out toilet paper? Give someone extra? Good luck with the jealous rage and impulse-control issues.

The female trainee stopped by the showers, careful not to look inside. The whole block watched. She was young, and three inmates had already told me they had a thing for redheads.

We had the standard conversation.

How long have you worked here?

Do you like it?

Do you know what's for chow tonight?

What's the deal with these pants?

The normal stuff.

A young inmate came up. Butted right in. And said, "Heyyy. Can I ask you a question?"

"That is a question."

"Oh dang, she got attitude!"

"No, just no time."

"Yeah, I like girls with attitude"

"I'm not a girl. And I'm on a mission."

"Your hair looks nice. How do you do it? How do you do it?"

She walked off with her clipboard to check windows and doors.

He said, "There goes a bitch."

He looked at me maybe hoping for a smile or laugh, as if our maleness was enough to agree on something.

I winced and scanned the shower instead.

He went off to sulk.

After two hours I closed up the showers and Flint told me to answer the phone and make the block announcements. That was a first. Most sergeants were protective of the PA system.

So I got to hear my voice over the PA call, *Chapel open, if you're going to chapel, go now,* and, *Return to your cells to prepare for the meal line.*

Inmates actually listened.

And after they went for their spaghetti and garlic bread, she let me announce the big one: *Count time. Count time. Be standing. Be visible. Lights on!* Our first count that evening.

Doors shut. Lights came on.

She said, "Good." And grabbed a count sheet. Another first. I never once saw a sergeant count. The roving female guard with something like fifteen years in counted with her. When I first came to the jail to get new-hire mandatory shots, she had processed me through the front door. She warned, "Working with the inmates is easy. It's staff that make it hard."

I said, Wow.

Flint stopped and chatted at several cells. She nodded and looked serious and took notes.

Back to the desk, she told me to call in the count, and said, "Had to check on the men. The only drama is Melvin. As usual. He's my project."

She got him out of his cell to count toilet paper rolls in the supply closet. He sat cross-legged and built TP towers.

"Have to keep him busy," she whispered. "I don't care how many rolls we have. It gets him to take a nap. He needs that too."

Then she told me to go and eat.

So I went and ate.

Which left three female guards alone.

With two hundred penises.

~

AT the lunch table, guards asked if we:

Had done each other's hair?

Had had a slumber party?

Had synced our menstrual cycles?

I ate quickly to escape and walked back on the block to three female officers updating the population board, escorting inmates to the laundry room, and making block announcements.

I was on shower duty again. But no longer tense. They were obviously better guards than me.

Post-nap, Melvin came up and said, "I been a man since always."

Awesome. How did you know?

"I brought a butcher knife to school and held it to a kid's neck."

But why, Melvin?

"He tested me."

That was a tough one to respond to. So I didn't. But I looked this up after shift. It was true. He did it. This event got him placed into the group home.

He ran off to tell others about being a man.

Finally, I got to close the showers and checked in at the bubble. The Attitude Guard said, "You smell like clean inmate."

Hah.

Flint sat me down to run the phone so she could make a round. She told me, "Don't let Melvin bully you."

Hah.

Roving Guard came through and asked, "You going to sit there all night?"

Hah.

But before she took three steps away a young inmate approached. I was embarrassed for him before he spoke.

"Heyyy. My question is why? Why work here?"

"Better than sitting in the dump truck I used to drive."

"Serious. How do you do it?"

"Well, you know, I just sort of clock in and do my job."

"You should be an actress."

"True. I pretend to be civil to annoying kids."

"I'm only here for a year. Could I call you when I get out?"

"Look, kid, you are kid number twenty thousand who has said the same kid shit to me. You even know where you're at?"

"What do you mean?"

"Didn't think so."

She walked off and out of a cell nearby there was a "Psssst. Hey. Psssst. Heyyyyy. Heyyyyyyy!" Which didn't seem to register.

I too wanted to know how she did it.

But it was count time and I heard, "A bitch says, 'Count time, count time, be standing, be visible.'"

That was Melvin with some drive-by bullying.

I announced, *Count time, count time, be standing, be visible.*

Inmates stood. Guards counted.

At the bubble afterward: no card games. Instead, Flint talked about raising horses. "The most dangerous part is the hay," she said. "If the hay is wet when you put it in the barn, even a little bit, it will give off nitrogen. Then the heat of the barn, that's all it takes. You have a firestorm. I've seen many a barn burn down."

Then we had some yelling down-range on Melvin's end.

Flint walked over.

Someone yelled, "You let Melvin out during lockdown! Why is he so damn special?"

Which made five others yell at him, protective of Flint.

She snuffed it. No misconducts or goon squads. Just a few calm words. A few listens. A few minutes to let things hang in the air to dry.

But of course Melvin the convicted arsonist lived there. He yelled, "I'll cut your fucking head off! I done it before!"

And the whole barn went up.

Flushed

A BLOCK'S shitter was a cramped hotbox by the phones and only worth risking on cool days.

BA's shitter was downstairs by the laundry room. You could squeeze in if you hunched and didn't mind the laundry guys knocking about next door. Good luck not minding—they drummed the tables and kicked the cabinets and did seemingly everything but laundry.

BB's shitter, the one in the sex offender block, doubled as a supply closet. After you.

BC's was BB's. Seriously, you first.

CA had nothing.

CB's worked like A's hotbox. So it didn't.

D block's shitter did not exist. But there was a urinal out in the open for anybody to use. And that was not happening.

The yards had urinals against the blocks. No dividers, and no thanks.

The education building was great until the big dude you wrote up the week before pulled up next to you and said, "You all right, CO. I knew you were just compensating." Then you see him look down at what you're holding. He said, "What's the problem? You stripped me six times."

The problem was that he kept count.

The infirmary/mental health unit's was okay. It looked normal if somewhat small. But the whole area smelled like shit. So it felt like you were stepping in right when somebody stepped out. And people screeched. And guards jingled keys while walking by the door. And nurses rolled carts by. And there was no calm.

So I didn't shit in jail for over a year.

~

I STEPPED into A block's once with stomach cramps. But the moment I sat, people kicked the door. They rattled the doorknob. They shuffled feet outside. They said, "Hurry up" and "What are you doing in there?" and "Number two? Number two? Are you making a number two?" And I was good. Cramps cured.

Then I walked up on the ranges and saw an inmate with headphones plugged into his TV. He draped a sheet over his clothesline, creating a kind of second room. I asked what he was doing. He didn't hear me. I waved my hands until he saw me. He said, "Gonna feed the warden." He lit incense (jail speak for cinnamon stolen from the kitchen and rolled into a cone). And I was bitter. He had complete sensory barriers there. Privacy.

But then E block happened.

E's shitter should not be called a shitter. That defiles the experience of using it. It was bright, had good ventilation, and the toilet had a good, strong flush. Just the size of it, huge for jail, something like eight feet by eight feet, was extravagant. It even had a real mirror—not just a piece of metal bolted to the wall.

~

AN extra fence separated E block from the main walks. The two hundred low-security inmates living there needed a pass to get through. Special passes for special inmates.

Melvin would never live there.

Being ticket-free for a year got a guy on the block. That and having less than two years left on his sentence. They were all short-timers except for four friendly lifers.

And the guards, they had to be special too. Blessed by Captain Grace. No block-banned officers allowed, even for one shift.

The building was newish, reddish, and niceish, unlike the rest of the joint. And there was air-conditioning. And a TV across from the officer's desk. And sunlight, actual, real sunlight coming through two thirty-foot window walls.

I still beat through all the jobs and their shitty shitters: yard, D block, A block, any block, but my name came up for E block more and more on the roll-call sheet. And for the first time since hitting a year in, I felt that jail accepted me.

And the thing was: I was proud of that.

I seemed destined to either work with the locked-down, head-sick men of the Mental Health Unit (MHU), or with the low-security, special men of E block. My weeks were split, two days in each, then a day or two in the yard.

~

FOR the MHU (pronounced "moo" in jail speak), I clocked in with Neck Beard, a guard who once fought a man over a parking spot at Walmart. He worked the unit full-time. I filled in for his partner's days off.

He told me, "Hot wings are basically dog food. Really, they are. And Grace has you here on a trial basis."

I asked if he had any advice.

He said, "It helps if you lose your shit and start screaming from time to time. Your turn for showers."

So I showered them one at a time. Squirted them with the gallon soap-shampoo-all-in-one bottle. Even handed them a towel afterward because it was too dangerous to have hooks inside the shower cage.

Then I patrolled the yard until the end of the week when I clocked in with Stokes on E. He was a slick-haired, false-teeth-wearing oldhead about to retire. On my first day with him, he said, "To get in here full-time, it helps if you cup Grace's balls. Take your time with it. Settle in. You can't just swallow his whole gun right off. Wear kneepads."

Then he said, "Check out our shitter."

And I knew right then which block I wanted.

~

I HUNCHED over the MHU monitor straining to see what was happening in the odd-shaped cells. One was a long triangle, another some kind of five-sided diamond, another a narrow rectangle, all different, like they were afterthoughts in the building process. On the monitor I saw an anorexic arm pawing around from under a bunk. He smeared feces in a kind of a circular pattern. He made little feces waves, little feces hills, little feces rainbows.

I asked Neck Beard if we needed to do something.

He asked back, "And what would that be? Take a sample?"

~

I STRETCHED and stepped into E's bathroom whenever I wanted. Stokes sat at the guard's station, always reclining in the barstool-height chair. The station looked like a terminal counter in any airport in America: Formica countertop, uniformed people behind it talking on the phone, a line of people standing in front.

I wandered through the block at ease and Stokes said, "Get to know the guys. They'll be nice. They have it good."

Inmates came up to me and said, "Hi. Nice to meet you."

~

MHU people I didn't understand lounged around on painted concrete looking at me looking at them.

A suicide attempt got a guy in the unit. Or a negative habit, like sexually assaulting toilet-paper rolls in the open.

One of the caseworkers told me, "We take inmates with acute or repetitive emotional dysregulation."

After a pause, she added, "You know, the crazies."

I looked at Neck Beard.

He said, "Shower time. Getting horny yet?"

After showers, I rolled the food cart to the cell doors. I made sure the dysregulated walked to the food slots with empty hands. I thought of my first interview—body-fluid fastballs. Then pushed trays of meatloaf at them. Most had long fingernails. No nail clippers allowed. One inmate had cups on the floor all around his bunk. "They're traps," he told me. "For you." He was the floor painter. He slept under his bunk. The cups were full of shit and piss. I held my breath.

Two trays of meatloaf sat on the cart for me and Neck Beard. We couldn't leave.

~

I took a deep breath of E block air. Not one trace of smoke. Inmates went outside for that.

Stokes asked for a volunteer to vacuum the carpet by the front door. Six inmates ran down. Stokes told them, "Get off my knob."

At least a quarter the E block guys worked outside the fence. One went out to jail's main sewage line every night. A screen in the line caught the big stuff flushed down that day: sheets, clothes, chip bags, any contraband disposed of in a hurry, like a porn mag. He raked it off. One night he said there was a dead cat on the screen. "Somebody flushed it," he said. "It had to come from inside."

I willed Grace to put me in E block. And when I saw him, I said . . . nothing. Just tried not to slouch. I wondered which block he would choose for me. And why. I did a lot of thinking in the E block escape pod. That's what I called the bathroom. It was a temporary reprieve, a furlough from it all.

~

UNDER the MHU fluorescent lighting, behind a metal door behind another metal door, a big guy head-butted the glass by the bubble and broke it. I wasn't there that day.

Neck Beard said, "I really lost my shit when he did that. Your turn for showers. Then programs."

I showered them. Then watched them play Yahtzee with the case-worker. Trap Inmate, cuffed and shackled, kept looking under the table at the caseworker's crotch. She terminated the session. I escorted him back to his door, tugging on his upper arm because he dragged his feet and smiled and smiled at the worker. I felt my face go red. It was the first time I had to physically restrain an inmate. I was glad he was small. He lay back down under his bunk and gathered around his traps. He said, "I'll know if you been in here fingering me again."

I walked by an observation cell and saw Melvin sitting on the bunk. I asked him what was up? He said, "I'll do it. I'll off myself. Tell them." He was on suicide watch.

Tell who? I asked.

"Them. You. You're them."

I saw him cycle from suicide watch to bucket to back. After CA he was nothing but tantrums and tears. He was no fun anymore.

Which made me realize he never was.

Why did I ever look to him for interest and entertainment? I wasn't the only guard who encouraged his behavior.

He asked, "Do you want to adopt me?"

This made me laugh. The surprise of it. Which made him cry. Which made my chest do something like collapse. That was the feeling. I went concave.

I mumbled Sorry and said I'd see if someone could talk to him. I made sure he was sleeping the next time I walked through. I wanted to tell Neck Beard about it, but he was trying to convince the caseworker that hot wings had ruined America.

~

STOKES said, "If I could stay on E, I wouldn't retire."

Guards had two-year limits on blocks. This kept them from getting too close to the inmates. Or from making too many enemies. He was near the end.

He said, "You been taking care of Grace, right?" He made a handjob gesture.

~

I GOT married. Our artist friend led the ceremony. We line-danced to "September." The strip-search-bought Mexican resort was all-inclusive. It had a marble bathroom. I went from watching Trap Inmate drink from his cups one day to ocean kayaking, snorkeling, and eating seafood-stuffed chili peppers the next. It was like E block.

When I clocked back in at jail, Stokes was retired, and I took his place full-time.

Grace never said a word to me.

And I had responsibility, finally, and a sense of inclusion. A guard's worth was measured by the job he worked. Up until then, my purpose in jail seemed to be to show up on time, sober, with my jail hat.

At home, my wife—that's what I called her then—talked about the future. We were a success. We opened individual retirement accounts. I was an E block full-timer. Cadre. Unit management. She was working on her dissertation, close to the end. We laughed and shared bottles of wine. Even though I had lost my wedding ring in the ocean on the honeymoon, and avoided thinking about the symbolism of that, we could afford a new one!

And we had a good meal in the dining hall. Real turkey. And real cornbread. I ate and celebrated, then walked into the quiet calm of the bathroom. Actual quiet. And actual calm. I was satisfied. And relieved.

I stepped out and Screen Scraper walked up with his splattered pants. He said, "This is your house now, boss. Congrats."

Thanks.

"But you're still jail."

And, actually, there was another silent treatment at home. Something about me calling her short. Repeatedly. But she was. Short. Didn't she know? I was just giving her shit. Repeatedly. It worked with the inmates.

Hecho en E Block

MARIGOLDS are rugged. The proof sparkled outside E block. Every spring the inmate grounds crew lined the sidewalk with them. And there, in the rocks and spit and cigarette butts, over summer, those fresh little unflowered weeds grew and budded into thigh-high bushes with a dozen golden heads each.

Late my second summer in jail I walked between them, dragging my fingertips through their frills. They glowed.

~

I STEPPED through E block's climate-controlled and filtered-air threshold to a line of inmates. Tuesday meant commissary.

The building was divided into three sections: A, B, and C, with six communal bathrooms. A side had two ranges with cells along the wall—more like rooms. Instead of bars, they had doors. Inmates even had their own keys. B side consisted of five barracks-style rooms with rows of bunk beds. We called them dorms—the biggest held thirty. C side was a mirror of A.

For some reason drywall was installed throughout. So there were body-part-shaped holes in half the walls: fists, elbows, heads.

An inmate with no front teeth and wearing thick-framed jail-issue glasses stepped to the desk. He said, "How about that pass?" Then he gave a loud laugh. "Haw. Haw. Haw."

Forty other guys hung by the desk waiting for the same thing. I gave Loud Inmate and the next three guys in line commissary passes. I took the rest of the group's ID cards and told them they would be called.

Me and Smolarski ran the block for second shift. Smolarski was a small, forty-something lifer in the National Guard. That seemed like a hard life: guard during the week, guard during the weekend. But he made the best sweet tea in the jail and was the great collector of sheets. He said, "Howdy," and while I stacked the IDs he dragged a recliner-sized laundry bag behind him to reclaim any extra sheets, pillows, or blankets inmates had hoarded. He filled it from just one dorm and yelled behind him, "Mine! All mine!" Then went outside for a smoke.

~

BEFORE Stokes left, I never worked with Smolarski. I filled in for him on his off days. Stokes told jokes, but Smolarski taught me the block. Call it pruning.

We exchanged sheets on Mondays. Ran commissary on Tuesdays. Moved inmates on Wednesdays and Fridays. Did cell and dorm checks on Saturdays. Handed out socks on Sundays. And every shift there were two yards, one meal, two counts, two medication lines, passes to write, a logbook to log, a phone to answer, rounds to round, announcements to announce, and inmates who needed. They needed clothes from the laundry room, or a new ID card, or their phone card fixed, or a new blanket because they spilled their coffee again, or their cell opened because they forgot their key, or a mop because the bathroom was flooding, or stitches because someone punched them right in the eyebrow and it split wide open like the drywall in dorm 3. All of it easy stuff.

We kept the schedule. The routine ruled us. It felt like a no-tips service-industry job.

~

LOUD Inmate came back from the commissary with a full paper bag. I called the next inmate from the stack of ID cards.

All of E's inmates had jail jobs. That was part of the deal for living there. They planted flowers, plowed the parking lot, stained underwear in laundry, and were transforming the cannery into some kind of commissary warehouse. All max-rate jobs: seventy-nine cents an hour, minus taxes. So after paying fifteen dollars for cable, having money deducted for victims' compensation (when necessary), an inmate had sixty dollars, easy, left over each month for the commissary. That bought a lot of soups on Tuesdays.

Loud Inmate walked outside with a fresh pack of Kite. I learned his name was Conway. And something happened as soon as I did: I saw him everywhere, like Melvin. He stood out from the unknown inmates. New car syndrome for people. Later I made a round and found him in a dorm he didn't live in. He was lying on a bunk, pretend-asleep. I shook my keys to pretend-wake him up. He said, "I was waiting to trade for some chips. Must've fell asleep. Haw."

Then an hour later, he lay in the same spot, but it was Sticky Buns that time. He followed me. I should have written him up. But gave him a warning instead.

At the desk, Smolarski said, "Howdy. Guess what Conway is in for?"

I guessed, Fraud.

Smolarski said, "Cat burgling."

Conway said, "True. Haw. Haw."

I left to make a round.

~

THE block had real ficus trees, single-man showers, a reading room, its own laundry room, an ice machine, a hot-shot (jail speak for hot-water dispenser), and tables with checkerboards printed on top. They weren't the standard you're-in-jail metal tables.

Scrabble was the block favorite. Bluffing was as important as vocabulary. I walked by a game. One guy said, "Go ahead, look up 'chillaxing.' Do it. Lose your damn turn."

I made it a game to learn all the names on the block.

It seemed like most inmates wanted to be invisible to the cops. And that was easy to do. A and D blocks held over four hundred each. And inmates moved from block to block constantly. So did the guards. If I worked a week on a block, I learned just a few names—and those were usually the guys who did something wrong (or they were Melvin). But on E, I was determined to keep the changing two hundred straight. I started right then.

Hunter was a quiet young kid who had a teardrop tattoo under his left eye. He lived in dorm 4, bottom bunk, and his dorm mates said he spent all night, every night watching the *Girls Gone Wild* infomercial over and over. Stifler was the only white guy in the otherwise all-black dorm 3. He laid on his bunk, a top bunk, for twenty-three hours a day. He didn't have a TV, only

left for meals. Dymeck lived on C side, first floor, and ran an unauthorized
fantasy football league. Probably cost twenty Kite to get in—big money.
Gomez, a short Puerto Rican, was maybe an inch taller than Melvin. Stokes
had named him Knee-High. He smiled and smiled and didn't speak much
English. Weber, who called himself Roach, lived in the only cell on the block
with its own toilet. He worked on the grounds crew and had a cock tattooed
on his forearm. He said, "It's a knife." It didn't look like a knife. Roach watered the marigolds at night and pulled off any wilting, browning blooms.
Above Roach lived two powerlifters. Verbitski had the bottom bunk, his
celly, Fox, the top. Fox told me, "Cretins come from the island of Crete."
Then he said, "At a minimum, you have to do the big three: bench, squat,
deadlift." Skinny guys seemed to bother him. Verbitski was a type 1 diabetic
and went into diabetic shock every other week because he would let his
sugar get too low. He looked at my body and said, "And shoulder presses
wouldn't hurt either."

Smolarski called out name after name on the PA.

I put faces to them as he called.

"Verbitski, you're up."

"Stifler on deck."

"Dymek in the hole."

Then it was mealtime.

Then count.

Then a walk past the flowers at the end of the shift.

Then a walk past them again the next day.

Then a month-long blur walking past the flowers to hand out socks and
commissary passes.

They grew and grew.

~

I WENT home to my wife crying on the couch. The cause: our laundry
basket. It was cracked. I nodded at her acute emotional dysregulation, com-
miserating with the emotional pain that a broken three-dollar basket could
cause. And I knew something was off. The MHU caseworkers had drilled
me to "Take note of sudden changes in behavior." I ran to the store for a
pregnancy test. Didn't even change out of my uniform. And it turned out,
according to the timing, we had made a baby somewhere down in Mexico.

We temporarily named the baby *Hecho en México*. And the marriage became a structured world of doctor's visits, vitamins, and Kegel exercises. Instead of an extended honeymoon I learned about mucus plugs.

~

ON the block, after everyone's name, I memorized numbers. All two hundred. I liked the game. From the desk I watched four different guys knock on Knee-High's, FX7304's, door in one hour. So I headed up to see what I could see in his room, but was delayed around the corner by Groth, FF9278, and Williams, FG6246, doing pullups on the stairs. I said, Take it to yard. Near them Conway, CX0055, played pinochle. "Haw. Haw." I took one step up the stairs and heard "Whoop, whoop." Inmates made that sound to impersonate a cop car siren to warn each other that jailcops were rounding. I didn't see anybody up top. But in the bathroom Rosa, FF9736, and Colón, GS5177, looked guilty. Rosa had hair clippings all over his shoulders. Haircutting on the block was against the rules. I told them to clean up and pay their one dollar at the barber shop. When I made it to Knee-High's room, I didn't see anything obvious from the door. He smiled and said, *"Hola, CO."* I told him I wanted to perform a fire and safety check. He said, *"No problema, CO."* It was clean—most Puerto Ricans took care of their stuff—the bunks were made, the rugs on the floor looked new. Maybe he had a few too many, but I didn't care about rugs. I was looking for gambling tickets or whatever it was drawing inmates to him. I didn't see anything, said thanks, and left. He smiled and said, *"De nada, CO."* I walked toward the stairs and bathroom and heard *"Bajando"* from downstairs. That's the Spanish warning for "coming down." Originally I thought they were calling me a *pendejo* (Spanish for "asshole"). I walked past the stairs to check the bathroom again: empty and clean. Right next to it was the sheet room. I unlocked it for the workers. Monday meant sheet exchange. Somebody had hung three towels on the rail to dry. I said, If these are here in one minute, they are mine. Colón sprinted out of his cell and grabbed them. Next I cut through dorm 4—whoop, whoop—four guys played cards on a bunk. I saw tear-drop-faced Hunter, GA2309, under a blanket, catching up, no doubt, from a long night of watching girls who went wild. I checked the bathroom on the other side: empty and filthy. I made a note to talk to the block worker then walked into dorm 3. Stifler, GE7774, was up there alone, not reading, not sleeping, just staring at the ceiling. I told him that he could be a monk. "Maybe," he said. "But reincarnation is bullshit." I walked out the back door—whoop, whoop—Verbitski, BU1688, the powerlifter said, "Maybe front squats. Try them. They'll fix your core." Fox, DF4091, said, "Really, though, you should do something. Anything." He wasn't joking. I walked down the stairs—*bajando*—Dymek, DN8644, the fantasy football guy, said, "Never draft a quarterback with your first pick. Never ever." I spent more time with them than I spent with my made-in-Iowa wife. We briefly talked baby names. She tested her students on the use of the imperative while I told Rebar, GG2525, You will wait your turn to smoke. Two Scrabble games with audiences got loud. I walked around the corner again to check on the sheet room—whoop, whoop—and saw Roach, EJ3182, stopped halfway down the stairs carrying an armload of sheets. I was gone for three minutes and that cock-armed, flower-picking Roach thought he could steal three rolls of sheets.

And the game wasn't a game anymore. I wrote him up.

~

WALKING through a dorm I knew exactly who didn't belong (Presence in an Unauthorized Area). I noticed a branch broken off of a ficus tree (Possession of Contraband? Weapon?). A few more weeks in, Colón called me "Super Cop." He said, "You seem different." I was finally enlightened, holding them accountable. A full-blown guard. A born-again hardass.

Thank Roach, I said.

An inmate on C side left his boots outside his door one night during count, and I tripped over them. I told him to take them in. He did. But the next night they were out again. And I told him to take them. And he did again. But the next night, there they were. So I took them and threw them in the trash.

They weren't boots anymore. They were rebellion. And I quashed it. He put in a grievance, and a few days later a lieutenant who was missing his front teeth like Conway called me up. He said, "I can see taking state boots. But not a privately owned pair."

I told him I didn't take them.

He yelled into the phone, "I didn't ask you if you took them!" And hung up.

That was it. Nobody could prove I took the boots. Nobody saw or admitted to seeing me take them. A few words and a short outburst from my superior declared my victory.

Congratulations, that phone call said, I had successfully abused my power.

But I blushed while hanging up the phone. Smolarski looked at me strangely. I went home and sulked. My wife asked what was wrong. I told her I was tired.

Jail speak for ashamed.

~

UNTIL then I had made plenty of naïve mistakes. In D block showers my first month, I saw a young inmate standing on top of the maintenance closet in there. I told him, Yo, get down.

He said, "Sorry, looking for my shampoo," and ran out. I handled it nice and sternly. This is what it meant to be a corrections officer I felt: we handled criminals. But four months later during a jail-wide shakedown a guard found two shanks up there. That's where that inmate was stashing them. I was bothered by it. Still am. Why didn't I stop that guy? Why didn't I search?

But with those boots, not even close to as dangerous as two shanks, I felt worse. The inmate knew. So all the inmates knew. A lieutenant knew. And Smolarski asked, "Did you take them? Not judging. Just so we're on the same page."

I told him No, and there in the most relaxed of jail environments, I sat stiff and embarrassed for a shift.

~

BUT for only a shift.

It was jail. I blamed the inmate for making me an asshole. He tested me and lost. Smolarski even seemed to embrace it, ready to lie for me.

Jail, the great enabler.

But years later I realized that this was the incident that germinated a different—Melvin might call it a more honest—me. I took my first step into little goon territory. I knew the difference between right and wrong. And chose the wrong. People go to jail for that.

~

BUT no one left anything outside his cell anymore. The next night, while I scanned the spotless block, not even a hand towel hanging from the rails, me feeling not one bit soiled, Verbitski walked by, dragging his feet and staring off in the distance. I watched him take slow step after slow step up the stairs. Fox met him halfway and looked down at me. After a long while they made it to their cell. But as soon as I made the announcement for count time, Fox came running down and said, "He's having a seizure!"

Smolarski shouted, "Shit!" And sprinted up to their cell.

I put my gloves on and grabbed a tube of glucose—sugar gel, grape flavored—from the closet and speed-walked to his cell. I twisted off the cap and force-fed Verbitski, that shaking and sweating big man who had a powerlifter's grip on the leg of his bunk, back to reality. He sucked the tube like a baby bottle. The phone rang, probably the control center wanting to know the count. But instead of letting them know that, yes, we still had 198 more inmates on that block than guards, I was squeezed into a room with 260 pounds of seized muscle.

All he said was, "Fuck."

He blinked. It must have been a bad feeling to come to and see me standing over him with the gloves on, because I had just had my fingers in his mouth. And he was still in jail. And it blew. Even with ruffled yellow flowers, an ice machine, air-conditioning, and all.

~

A DAY later Conway stood at the hot-shot, yelling, "Yes, I'm eating mighty big tonight! Haw. Haw." He had two soups, not one.

I asked him to keep it down.

He turned on me and said, "I'm not a child. I'm a man. And you are going to talk to me like a man!"

Then, as he walked to his dorm, he pretended to shoot at me five-year-old style with his hand: bang, bang.

Three months of letting him slide and he gave me that pistol-shaped thank you in front of the entire block. I wondered if it was because of the boots. I cuffed him—click, click. The ticket: Threatening Employees and Refusing to Obey an Order.

Two soups sent Conway to the bucket.

The E block honeymoon was over.

But those marigolds sure were nice. I admired them on my way to the property room with Conway's possessions in garbage bags. He'd get his stuff back when he paroled from the bucket. The flowers were ruffled and thriving, each bloom the size of a fresh-rolled pair of inmate socks.

Then the grounds crew came through the next day and ripped them out of the ground for winter.

Chickenshits

DRIVING the main drag through town took us past an inmate. He wore pa-role clothes: jeans and a jean jacket. Both four sizes too big, with industrial creases. He smoked a hand-rolled cigarette. In his pocket, no doubt, he had a bus ticket back to whatever county sent him upstate. I didn't recognize him. One of the fatherless eighteen hundred that didn't live on E block.

I pointed him out to my wife.

Look: inmate.

She asked, "Who? How do you know."

Wasn't it clear? He might as well have been running down the side-walk in shackles and cuffs. But the people around him didn't seem to no-tice either. A group of college students walked by chatting.

His jacket flapped in the wind. We drove on, but I watched him in the rearview mirror.

Smolarski told me to not think about jail on my days off. "Clock out completely."

Right. Didn't even make it twelve hours.

But the plan for the day: coffee, midwife, karate class. Quality time in the middle of the week since I had worked the last three weekends.

With our coffee—decaf for her, she well past showing—I sparred her for the seat with its back to the wall. And won.

My wife suggested we write a book together. We both read a lot, and she said I wrote funny letters. So we talked plotlines. What would the book be about?

Fiction, definitely. She likely suggested some intelligent and culturally important concepts involving identity or gender stereotypes. But all I knew about was working lousy jobs and being mad. So that would have to be it. We gave the protagonist a name: Gary. And Gary is a guy who is an expert at working many meaningless jobs. He is actually addicted to quitting jobs. The feeling he gets from quitting, that must be the high heroin users chase. That's how good it feels.

Anyway, there's Gary's father, he's a programmer. Good with robots.

And there's Gary's mother. One of Gary's earliest memories is asking his mother about all the orange bottles in the cabinet and hearing her answer, "They're for balance."

Totally fictional. Character backstory and development.

And some people bother him so much he feels sick.

A boss who eats blocks of cheese like sandwiches does it.

So does another boss who, when he speaks, repeats himself three times.

Mostly bosses have this sickening effect.

Or people who tell him what to do.

Totally fictional. Just ideas over coffee.

Gary wants to create a reality TV show. The concept: he takes jobs just to quit them. Work itself never bothered him. Just boss behaviors. One boss called him a different nickname every day, like: my guy Gary, Gary the gangster, and so on, for nine months. Maybe the climax of the season would be him finding the one grind he could stomach. And him staying there. The rare single-season show. What would a good title be?

Purpose?

While we brainstormed, me trying not to scare my wife too much, a guy two tables down distracted me with his gnawing. His mouth open, he crunched down hard on some chips. Eating like Melvin.

But the idea was for Gary to find ways to subvert the companies. Bring down the unkind ones somehow. This concept is shallow in the notes. No specifics. And really, how could you get companies to act right? We have jails full of people who can't act right. Maybe through scenes? Like maybe show the shift bosses at a warehouse standing at the timeclock forcing loaders to clock out the second they left the floor.

No, you cannot go to the bathroom.

No, you cannot get a Band-Aid.

Clock out. Clock out. Clock out.

If you show what needs changed, will it change?

Gary also wonders about life. The book would clock him out for balance. Can't be too serious all the time. Gary hates movies that are too serious. And bosses. Gary imagines the bug population explosion we would have if everyone stopped driving for just one year. Count the dead bugs on your windshield. Multiply by everyone. The resulting pestilence would be like in A block's maintenance tunnels.

My wife or I typed the session. Me, judging by the grammar and spelling. Her strategy was probably an attempt to get me to act right. Obsess over something nonjail for a while. I got stuck in the routine of it all: six days on, two days off. My free time: talking with guards about jail. My unfree time: talking with guards about jail while in jail. That week's topic: the guard beat up during breakfast. And here we thought French toast was a good meal. An inmate punched the guard from behind while he was unlocking a gate. Good news, though, you could barely see the staples it took to close his scalp.

Fiction needed.

I hit save on the book file. We drove to the midwife's office. Bugs all over the windshield. Greasy mass murder.

The baby's heart sounded like someone energetically eating jail-brand Doritos. Melvin wouldn't let me clock out.

But look at this togetherness. We drove to dinner. Thai food. I had never even tried the stuff until she introduced me to it. Prewife, dollar menus were all I knew. I looked for the parolee. There didn't appear to be any carnage on the sidewalk where I had seen him earlier. Next stop: karate class. I eyeballed a guy in the locker room. I knew him. It was a night-shift guard wearing shorts and a T-shirt. Looking fucking alien out of uniform.

Ten years earlier an inmate had knocked that guard out in the standard way: from behind. He awoke to inmate laughter. Standard too. He retreated to night shift. Expected. All the inmates were locked up at night. I worked with him one night and he said, "I'm thinking about making a comeback to days. I met a girl online." It sounded like, put me back in, I can hack it. But at one point, he sat completely still for twenty minutes. I asked him if he was okay.

He said, "I met a girl online."

The one time I saw him work a day shift was for mandatory overtime. When the lieutenant called his name for roll, he followed it with, "Welcome back to daylight, Chickenshit!"

The entire room laughed and laughed.

The chickenshit's mouth smiled. His everything else did not.

And he sat on a bench in the locker room drying his hair with a towel. I didn't bother talking to him. Figured he wouldn't recognize me anyway. I walked to the wrestling room, where we held class.

We bowed at the door when the master came in. We bowed to the flags. I led warmups. The class was full of promising college students. I couldn't relate. My wife did her pushups despite the belly. She would train right up until birth, kicking people in the head all the while.

I didn't take days off either. Had to save my vacation for the big day.

But the way it worked, me getting home around 10:30 p.m., my wife teaching at 8 a.m. We didn't align. She stayed up, sometimes, having food ready for me, but had to retreat to sleep shortly afterward.

So that left me alone to detox from jail in whatever way I could before being able to sleep.

Which sometimes meant playing a video game. For six hours. Or drinking a sixpack. Or going for a long run in the middle of the night. Or drinking a sixpack then running as an experiment. I wanted to see if I could run faster.

Nope.

But it hurt less.

I tried to clock out to music and weights in the basement. And angsty films. And by writing advice to myself in a notebook: *Try hard to ignore the feeling that you are playing dress up and swinging a foam sword.*

Coping mechanisms, I know these are called now. Looking for balance.

My wife hadn't given me a silent treatment in months. The baby business had her focused. Her purpose clear: she would mother this child in her typical driven fashion.

How nice, to have that vision.

I was scattered. I did martial arts whenever I could. Read books about it. I practiced breaking concrete. Concrete's hard, but brittle. Got good at it—fantastic party trick, by the way. I trained two other guards to fight. I was ready for a fight and could always best the other guards in wrestling and chokes. Very good at chokes. Too good. After choke nine a morning before clocking in, one of the guys raged and kneed me in the ribs. I had pain and popping noises in my side for six weeks. Was briefly addicted to ibuprofen because of this. Tried yoga. Tried handstands. Sucked at handstands. And yoga. Practiced juggling. Woodwork kept me busy—for a few weeks. The house filled with sawdust and stain fumes. One of the guards I trained suggested we try an extreme workout routine that leaves many of its practitioners injured.

Sure.

Ever search for purpose so hard you cannot sit still?

I tried everything but express emotions with words. Problem was, first you have to identify the emotions associated with a guard attacked with a stapler. How did I feel about that guard's skull fracture?

Just grumpy today, I told my wife. Just in a bad mood today.

Jail speak for stressed. Jail speak for scared.

Acting out is easier.

But cope too hard on your sparring partner and, snap, they no longer spar. They fight.

After warmups, karate class moved on to us fluidly slashing each other to pieces with wooden training knives. We aimed for tendons and arteries. The master gave a long talk about the mindset of a butcher. How the best butchers don't have to sharpen their knives because they know where to cut. No bone hits. All soft tissue. Do you know what a butcher sees when looking at people?

The inside.

Be a butcher.

Which made me fidget. We had had two recent attempted suicides at the jail. Both from short timers. There wasn't as much blood as I expected. And tendons are white. That was surprising. Karate was meant to distract me through punches and kicks.

Class ended. We bowed to the flags, drove home, and my wife went straight to bed. Long day for someone living for two.

I tried reading. But the book was too serious. I turned on a video game. One that let me be a criminal.

Word was that a new jail was going up on Rockview's property. It was going to be designed from E block's open floor plan. Great, was the sentiment among the guards. But the open floor plan will still restrain children, create chickenshits, and cause suicide. Because, really, the same people will be walking on it.

Outside of our townhouse, a guy stood on the sidewalk. Our block was dark. No reason to stand there. I paused the game and walked to the door. He had on a jacket and was going through his pockets.

I opened the door.

It was some college kid. He lit a cigarette and walked on. I watched him for a bit. Like everyone, that kid was one bad day away from jail. That's how easy it is to go. Because this is what I saw outside:

The inside.

A Jailcop's Glossary of
Terms for Jail Copulation

AMOEBAS: single-cell organisms.

The sick, the violents, and the chronically antisocial stayed in single cells. No celly for them. This lasted for months or years depending on behavior and modern medicine. HIV got a guy a single cell for the rest of his life. Reducing contact—making sex difficult—cut down on the spread of disease and its pricy medications. This was simple jail economics.

On night shift I saw a single-cell gunning for staff (jail speak for masturbating in front of staff). I saw him at 2 a.m. Then again at 4. Same position, on his bunk, legs spread, close to the bars.

I didn't stop. The other guards said something about him too. All night he did it. During the day he wore breasts, called them "boobies." They were Vaseline-filled officers' gloves (gloves probably taken from the trash, Vaseline from the commissary) that he put in hand-sewn pockets in his shirt. He had raped a girl, spent a decade in prison, got out, raped another girl, got another twenty-five years.

It made me tense that he was in the same county as my wife.

ATTRACTION: get together.

Proximity is the number one factor for initiating a relationship. It's not waist-to-shoulder ratio or nice teeth. It's proximity. At Rockview, couples met face to face. While playing softball: the pitcher and catcher hooked up. While serving breakfast: the sausage guy and the biscuits guy served it up. All it took was conviction and tight homosociality to lead to homosexuality.

AUTOEROTIC ASPHYXIATION: happy ending.

Inmate Welder killed himself on the toilet. He was a single-cell guy with the ninja (jail speak for HIV). There wasn't a note. Just a dead naked guy sitting on the toilet at 6 a.m. count. I don't know what he used around his neck.

Nobody said autoerotic asphyxiation while we talked about it over our grits and coffee. One jailcop said, "I understand killing yourself. But why naked?"

I said it was probably an accident.

He said, "Right. Just like how he accidentally shot that guy to get here."

I was surprised that no other jailcops considered dangerous masturbation a suspect.

A week earlier, Welder had told me, "Ever since I came up hot, everyone wants me. Losing weight made me sexy." He seemed happy.

BJ2055: the oldhead on the bottom bunk.

On a random overtime night shift, I made the early round at 10:15 p.m. When I walked by one cell on CA, I saw a short guy with a big head and scruffy beard facing his much older celly, who sat on the bottom bunk. It was obvious that I had just interrupted a blow job.

They acted nonchalant, like they were just chatting. Me too. I kept rounding, all nonchalant. I was supposed to look in cells to make sure people weren't cutting or hanging up. Plus I had to count them. But I didn't want a show.

I jingled my keys loudly while rounding from then on. Fair warning.

Afterward, that oldhead went out of his way to say hi to me around the jail. Like we had some connection. Maybe he felt he owed me because I didn't write them up. I don't know. He walked with a cane. He was friendly. His inmate number was BJ2055.

CELIBATE: a celly masturbating his celly.

COMING OUT OF THE CLOSET: first you need a closet.

Rockview didn't have many that inmates could access.

Cyprus, an athletic inmate, refereed the softball league. He lived in CB, and we talked once a week or so about the Philadelphia Eagles' state of affairs.

He took in a new, young inmate for a celly. They fell in love, got careless, got caught by a jailcop, and both went to the bucket. After that, Cyprus accepted his homosexuality. He had to. Everyone knew.

And once paroled from the bucket, Cyprus back on CB, his lover sent to another block, they still spent time out in the yard together, or in the library. That was devotion. In and out of the hole their relationship stood.

CONJUGAL VISITS: gay for the stay.

Rockview didn't have conjugal visits. But there was still plenty of sex. Guys could change cells every thirty days. All it took was a piece of paper with both inmates' signatures.

The form asks which bunk they prefer: top or bottom.

"Conjugal" means "having to do with marriage." Cellies spent twelve hours a day locked in together. Successful partnerships meant cellies could sit and not talk, give each other space in that lack of space, take turns with the chores (the rug shaking, the cigarette rolling), split the cable bill, and time bodily functions. They partnered up based on the law of attraction: proximity. Lifting partners, Bible studiers, and breakfast servers linked up.

But domestic disputes happened too: lovers one week, divorced the next. When I asked a forty-something tall white guy in for aggravated assault why he wanted a cell-change form, he said, with his eyes watering, "Mike told me to leave."

CRUISING: work.

It went on in the big yard with the two softball fields. Openly gay guys hung out on one set of bleachers close to Tower 4. Not many inmates stopped to talk to them out there. But that didn't mean that guys wouldn't approach them later in private, at their cell, or back in the kitchen while stirring gravy. Sitting on those bleachers was advertising. Some wanted love and chose their partners carefully. Others wanted to work their hustle (jail speak for side profession).

The world's oldest hustle.

EDUCATION: role models.

A father and son both did time for sleeping with the same thirteen-year-old girl. The father came to Rockview. He hung himself in the yellow-stained AC. Did it with a sheet on the bars.

Six months later, the son showed up. He didn't have his file, so he went to the AC. He knew that his father had killed himself there and asked to not have that same cell. He was given the one next to it.

The son became a long-time resident of the sex block. In there he took part in support groups, therapy sessions, weekly counselor meetings, and classes to keep him from reoffending. Inmates stayed until they graduated or failed. Sometimes it took years. Admitting to homosexual acts on the block caused immediate expulsion. Very few "out" inmates graduated.

I don't know the philosophy of the program or if it was effective. I never saw the son graduate.

ERECTILE DYSFUNCTION: heartache that keeps men down.

Viagra commercials warn, "Ask your doctor if your heart is healthy enough for sex."

Inmates said the jail food had saltpeter in it. Saltpeter is potassium nitrate. Supposedly it reduces the male sex drive. And supposedly it was in the scrambled-egg mix.

While I was in army boot camp, the same rumor went around. Except that the saltpeter was in the fruit punch. I believed it.

But after a month of pushups and marching, we got a sex education class from a lady who stuck her whole hand inside of a condom and said, "The 'the-condom-is-too-small' excuse isn't valid. Wrap it up." And she told us, "About your hard-on problems—yes, I know about them—it's the stress in your diet, and nothing else, that's responsible for the lack of blood flow. You'll get it back. Don't you worry."

If it works in jail—erectile function—what does that mean? That inmates aren't stressed?

That seems dysfunctional.

GAY: leaving early to spend time with the wife.

Near the end of fight night at the sports bar, two male mixed-martial-artists were locked in a grunting, north-south position (mixed-martial-arts

speak for a 69-like position). The jailcops with me yelled, "Punish him!"
They yelled, "Tear him a new asshole!"

After that fight I had to go. It was early. Not even the main event yet.
But my wife was leaving for a conference early in the morning and I wanted
to spend time with her. I stood up.

The jailcop next to me said, "Where you going?"

I told him.

He shouted after me, "Gayyyyyyyyyyyyyy!"

HOMOSEXUALITY: be warned.

In Pennsylvania, when inmates graduate from their county jail with a
guilty plea or verdict, they are sent to a sorting jail for the state. There, based
on race, gang affiliation, mental illnesses, disabilities, crimes, and behaviors,
they are assigned to their permanent-unless-they-fuck-up-again-and-get-
transferred state jail. They get a pamphlet on jail survival. It's two pages.
The title: *Eight Pitfalls to Avoid in Prison*. On drugs it says, "Drugs are for sick
people." On stealing: "The less you have, the less you have for someone
to steal." On sex: "If you choose to dabble in homosexual activity while
you're here, you'll be entering a ritualistic subculture that thrives on usury,
violence and modern-day slavery."

MEGAN KANKA: the victim that led to Megan's Law.

An ex-con fresh off a six-year sentence raped Megan Kanka, then murdered her, then raped her again.

She was seven.

And that little girl bit the hand of her murdering rapist so hard that the
mark she left was used as evidence at his new trial.

Now, sex offenders are required to give DNA samples in order to parole.
In Pennsylvania, they also have to complete the sex-offender program and
register with the state police.

Some refused the program. So they refused parole. And sex-offense
sentences are long. Rape is a minimum ten. A second sex offense goes for
twenty-five.

Will, the staff dining-hall server, was convicted for receiving a blowjob
from a fifteen-year-old girl. He was probably close to fifty, short, and asked
me every day, "How you doing today, sir?" When I asked him if he ever

got bored of his job, standing over the hot trays of biscuits that tasted like bootheels, he said, "Bored? Man, this is my life."

His sentence: four to nine years. He could have been out before I started at Rockview, but he refused the program. He said that the girl knew what she was doing. And he was going to serve all nine years to prove it.

PERVERTABLES: implements of masturbation.

After inmates adapted to jail life and their stress levels went down, a good tool for masturbation was a toilet paper roll with the cardboard core removed. Stuff in one of the baggie-type gloves the kitchen workers got and squeeze some Vaseline inside that. Insert body part. Wait for the whole deal to warm up, and it's just like the real thing, I was told. You control the tightness—rubber bands help with this.

Or if you score an officer's glove, turn it inside out. Inflate it. Pull the fingers through the middle and tie the thing shut—make sure the fingers are in the knot. And there you go. Now you have a balloon with five holes. Never use soap or shampoo for lube.

These are called fifis (jail speak for any inanimate object you can fuck).

PHONE SEX: if the phones were on, it was happening.

The phone-room cop could listen in on any inmate phone in any block. Inmates asked for money, begged for money, threatened for money, and had phone sex: "I'ma pull yo hair. I'ma slap yo ass." That sort of thing. The phone-room cop said, "It's boring." He carried around a pocket-sized book of psalms.

PORN: misconduct.

When I started, only pictures that showed penetration were considered contraband. Nudity was okay. But then one day Pennsylvania declared that any nudity was contraband, so we porn-raided the whole joint. Had to be a literal ton we took to the dump.

After that, the most popular magazine in jail became *Esquire*. *Jet* a close second. Both always had a lingerie or swimsuit spread. A legal one, by jail standards. Inmates cut them out, passed them around, and sold them.

PREDATORS: arresting doesn't mean stopping.

A lifer on CB block named Salt told me that some of the kitchen workers "be plottin' on" the new kid. Salt was talking about rape. And I'm pretty sure it was him doing the plotting. When the kid walked by, Salt licked his lips.

When his TV broke, he claimed that the weekly generator test burned it out. He said, "I don't have people on the street anymore," meaning people who would send him money for a new one. He knew how the system worked. There were dozens of TVs sitting in the property room from inmates who had left the jail. He went after the block sergeant hard. I walked by as he said, "Hey! Hey! Oldhead, don't fall asleep on me, this is serious!" He had lulled the sergeant to sleep—luckily the corporal running the desk was still alert and working the phone and PA system.

That's real jail life: inmates sitting around, plottin' on the establishment, boring everyone with their game.

But Salt got a new-to-him TV two weeks later.

His plots worked.

I felt bad for the new kid—I told his counselor that he needed a new job.

RAPE: it happens in jail.

This should surprise no one. Rape happens on the street, why not off? This is life. Whether it's a power thing: payback for being told when to eat, sleep, and shower. Or a reproductive-urge thing. Or a cultural thing. Or a family history thing. Or a whatever-the-reason thing, inmates did it. There are assholes on this planet. Welcome to Earth. Sometimes I feel sorry for the moon for having to face it all the time. The moon probably thinks, "I'm always attracted to the wrong type."

But.

Only once did I hear about an inmate reporting a rape (an oral rape that happened in the kitchen). The victim was a special-needs-type inmate with maybe an eleven-year-old's mentality living on a general-population block—one of the smaller blocks, but still too big for him. Another baby in jail.

REFORMED: no more tears.

A jailcop caught a guy with a teardrop tattoo at the corner of his eye straddling the face of a fat guy. Another jailcop caught another teardropped inmate shaving his celly's ass. Another teardropped inmate liked his cellies young, real young. Another teardropped inmate had used condoms in his footlocker. Teardrop tattoos often represent that a person has a body (jail speak for murder charge).

Jail: where the killers and lovers of men live.

SEXUAL MISCONDUCT: staff-on-inmate love.

The nurse was single and short and round and got caught because she brought in two cell phones.

The counselor was young and single and got caught because she brought three inmates into her office. Things happened with those inmates: train things. Her job ended because somebody felt left out and snitched.

The jailcop was short and friendly and got busted when FBI agents photographed her at a train station with a newly maxed out (jail speak for finished his sentence) skinhead.

Inmates don't get punished. It's not a crime to have sex with staff. Technically, staff members are in a position of power, so it's their fault. What inmates get is respect. What staff members get is a chance to resign. Criminal charges if not consensual.

SCREWS: jailcops.

This was a full-time occupation of many inmates: spinning the screws. The most effective technique to spin a screw involved being nice. That's it. Then asking for a favor. It starts small, with maybe a cigarette, then, before the guard knows it, he's bringing in heroin for fear of losing his job. Or so a bunch of "Welcome to Corrections" videos claimed. But, in reality, we had heroin at Rockview. Someone brought it in.

Any affection in that world was surprising.

I was more prepared to handle hate.

Nice was a sucker punch.

One career parole violator talked to me everywhere he saw me. He told me, "You know, before I came to prison and saw my uncle mopping the shower in A block, I actually believed he was in the CIA." But then he started asking for magazines and newspapers and books. He was only being decent because he wanted to spin the screw: me.

It should surprise no one that jailcops have trust issues.

SEXY JOB: it wasn't.

Looking at the distended belly of a hep-C-positive inmate wasn't sexy—
even if he was wearing shoe-polish eyeliner and his hips swung. Tobacco-
yellow-stained fingers from rolling cigarettes, Salisbury steak farts, infected
hemorrhoids (I think that's what I saw once)—not sexy—not even close.

Nothing got me less in the mood than waking up at 5 a.m., driving to
a hundred-year-old jail to change in the nonheated locker room with chew
wads sticking to the ceiling only to count inmates who didn't mind pissing
while I walked by.

Jail was not an aphrodisiac. A shower was self-mandatory after shift.
Before hugs. Before handshakes.

SOAP: a detergent meant for cleaning.

That joke about not dropping the soap in jail, that's all it is: a joke.
When all the guys were in the showers lathering up, jailcops monitored
them constantly.

Inmates wore their underwear—the state-issue white boxers—while
showering. If a guy was in there naked, it generally pissed off the other
inmates. They wore them for modesty. If I saw an inmate drop his soap, he
just bent down and picked it up. Nobody joked. In actual jail, the important
thing to remember about soap was to use it.

THE OL' IN 'N OUT: parole.

There were four or five jail-married couples at Rockview. The free
agents, the openly homosexual and single, were treated like meat. But the
couples were off the market.

On A block lived two short guys: Frank, a lifer, and Sean, a lifetime
reoffender. They were block workers. They celled right next to each other
in single cells. Frank was more social, and once when I walked by his cell,
he was boiling a cup of water for Sean's tea with his stinger. It was sweet.
Some inmates blew the block's fuses with stingers. But not Frank. He had
experience.

Both built relationships with the block cops. Frank was top worker. He
waxed the toilet seat to a shine in the staff bathroom. There was a floater
one day—and all he asked for was a jailcop's glove and got it down. Sean
offered me a cup of iced tea one night while I worked the front door of the
block. I declined. He seemed disappointed.

Frank shot a teenager in the back when he was twenty. I heard Sean went on some kind of drug-fueled joyride / crime spree across the state. He did it more than once.

They decorated the Christmas tree every year with tinsel and everything. D block's crooked tree just had sheets and toilet paper on it.

I doubt Frank and Sean had much sex when I knew them. Shrek told me that Sean used to be big, one of the muscle freaks out on the yard. Then he paroled. Many times. He went in and out of jail. He and Frank were apart for years at a time but always got back together. I only knew the skinny version of Sean. I'm sure he was HIV-positive. Didn't matter. Frank stayed loyal.

TIED AND BOUND: love.

In Spanish, the same word for is used for handcuff and wife: *esposa*. My wife doesn't think this is funny. But I see the connection. Inmates are involuntarily committed to jail. People involuntarily fall in love. Marriage is called a commitment. People are committed to jail. There are judges, rules, regulations, romance, jewelry, jealousy, sex, fights, stress, bedroom changes when it goes bad, tears, counselor visits, bedroom changes when it goes good, unrelenting proximity, sweet nothings, mean everythings, heartache, and maybe a few cups of tea during the good stretches.

Love is a cup of stinger-boiled tea—sure, that sounds right—it can be sweet or blow a fuse.

Jail-Bred

THE two hundred best inmates lived on E block—said the two hundred inmates living on E block. They called it the honor block. The going-home block. The free-to-roam block. And only the jail-good inmates came out to free-roam.

E block's counselor left their files behind the desk, so I saw what I worked with: third-degree murderers, five-DUI owners, aggravated assaulters, and one guy, an infanticider. He beat his girlfriend's three-year-old son to death, came to jail, and earned an undisputed spot on the volleyball team. Outside hitter.

How another one of the jail-good inmates made it to the honor block was what he did to a sixty-eight-year-old woman: he bludgeoned her with a baseball bat.

He came to jail with a life sentence, got a chapel job, stayed out of trouble for a few years, and it was official: he was good, inside-those-razor-wire-fences-good. He's probably still on that block. I hope he's proud. I hope he likes the marigolds. He could step on one and it'll bounce back. They're tough, like him. When he's holding a baseball bat.

Jail-good meant a guy had been ticket-free for one year and knew how to talk nice with staff. Counselors helped assign custody levels: one to five. Level 1's got halfway houses. Level 2's got the honor block. Level 5's got the bucket. And all the in-betweens, the 3's and 4's, 90 percent of the jail, needed to be nicer (jail-nicer) if they wanted to smell E block's flowers.

The guy who watered the marigolds came to E block because of what he did to a nine-year-old girl while babysitting: fingered her through her underwear.

His file was graphic.

And he was the top candidate for E block's head block worker, a coveted job because he got all the guard-brought-in real coffee he could drink.

He asked me, "You know what a mule is?"

I guessed, Drug smuggler? That was our context.

He said, "No. The animal, I'm talking about. It's half donkey. Half horse. Its own species. Big enough to carry weight. But small enough to be controlled."

Well, that's interesting.

He said, "Smart enough to listen to humans. But dumb enough to listen to humans."

I asked why he was telling me this.

He said, "But they can't reproduce. They're all sterile."

Um.

He said, "Nature's eunuchs. The result of forced crossbreeding. And that's how I feel in here."

Then he said, "Any word on that top block-worker job?"

I told him that it looked like it was his. Congrats.

Outside of jail, that kind of talk would probably get someone committed. But where people were already committed, that was small talk.

Four lifers lived on E block. Plus another two guys who were doing so much time that they would likely die in jail. And with those six guys who did something so terrible that they needed to be separated from free society for the rest of their lives, the worst of the worst on the outside, I appreciated their personable, friendly, and intelligent ways.

Kill someone with a kitchen knife while on a drug-fueled rampage?

Have a room to yourself. Take two mattresses. Take them because, here it is: jail is a different animal.

There was inside jail.

There was outside jail.

And I became their offspring.

X

I DROVE to jail, put on a uniform, and stuck out my chest. But only did that in costume. Right before shift, I was too shy to raise my hand in history class—my second attempt at higher learning. I blushed when the teacher called me anyway. Then I asked a man down for aggravated assault, On a scale from one to dumb, how dumb is you? But avoided eye contact with the professor teaching criminal justice—even though there were four hundred students in the lecture room. I learned that looking away meant, yes, that fingersmith-inmate did, in fact, steal the two T-shirts from the laundry-room table. I cold-sweat when a woman in a bar grabbed my arm and said, "I like them strong, tall, and silent." I mumbled something to her about being married. Then asked a murderer in a loud, clear voice, What are you going to do? Murder me because I won't write you a pass to yard? And I didn't blink. And grit on him until he broke eye contact. Then had zero clues on what to talk about with my mother-in-law. I sort of smiled at her joke about a dog. Then spent forty-five minutes discussing whether or not the Philadelphia Eagles had a realistic chance for a wild-card berth with a serial child-rapist and agreed with everything he said. I worried how a pimple looked while pumping gas before shift. But spilled coffee on my shirt on purpose just to see how many inmates would comment (thirty-eight). I laughed when a muscly, angry, habitual staff-assaulter called me an asshole. But raged when a middle-aged woman drove five miles per hour below the speed limit on the way home. Then felt intelligent when an inmate said, "For real? This is the twenty-first century?" Then felt idiotic when my wife's friend said, "I made focaccia. Would you like a piece?" And I asked, And what exactly is a "focaccia"? But understood what a Mexican who spoke no English wanted from a head nod a hundred feet away (his door unlocked because he forgot his key). But was lost despite listening to my wife as close as I could for thirty-five minutes and not being able to decide if she wanted me to get a vasectomy or adjust our savings account or replace the felt pads on the kitchen chairs because she kept saying "protection" and "returns" and "I'm not saying this is important, but this is important." I told one of my wife's advisors, Ever notice how killers look like everyone, so everyone looks like a killer? Then heard him say back, "Ahhh." But I said the same thing to a guard and he said, "Bro, ain't that some truth." And my wife's friend said, "You're quiet." And the inmates and guards said, "You have the gift of the gab with a temper." And when I heard a story about an inmate busted for giving blowjobs back at the rear door of the dining hall, how he squatted down in a trash can, popping up to blow guys and ducking down if the guard made a round, that was jail-normal. And when I stomped nine roaches it was just another day. And if I went home mad about an argument with a skinhead about the amount of shredded cheese on his tray on taco day my wife looked at me like, um. Just um. But maybe she didn't see the inside-out collision taking place on what felt like a genetic level. But probably she did. Years later, she claimed that she did. But for me, seeing a man scrubbing his heavy winter jacket while taking a shower made it a normal jail-Monday. And watching a guard punch the wall for being sent home because he wore black pants without the stripe, the piping, on the side, that was a normal jail-Tuesday. And having a guard show me his crushed middle fingernail—slammed by an eighty-pound cell door—jail-Wednesday. Too bad. Seriously, don't care. Followed by jail-Thursday, jail-Friday, and jail-Saturday when I fantasized about wrestling six different guys to the ground. And I used to be so nonviolent. But on jail-Sunday I worked a double shift and only fantasized about a job where I could sit down. Which I didn't get. Of course. Welcome to yard, fucker. Then I heard a woman outside jail tell a story about how she grew up in Texas and scorpions lived in the walls of her house. She said that they would fall from the vent above her bed at night. So she didn't sleep. Like ever. And I responded with absolutely no surprise. Normal jail stuff there. Scorpions everywhere. Sorry to hear it. But when I told her the trash-can blowjob story, she said, "Now that's fucked up." I earned a B in history. And an A in criminal justice—imagine that. My first ever college A. Then an outside-somebody told me, "You remind me of Clint Eastwood. Always angry." Then an inside-somebody said, "You remind me of my brother." Then my sister-in-law handed me a walking taco—a little Doritos bag loaded with meat and cheese and salsa and a fork—and I said, Jail food! Word, homey! And she said, "It's a walking taco." And I said, No, it's a handheld chichi. And she said, "What?" And I said, Yep. And she said, "What?" And I said, Yep. Then I transitioned without a transition to an army story about a soldier who had heatstroke during a fake war somewhere in Louisiana. The medics stripped him naked and tossed him onto a helicopter. But just as I got into the story, describing the red Louisiana clay matting down his hair, I had to censor the best detail: that the heat casualty, some eighteen-year-old low-IQ nobody from Alabama, sported a huge erection while he lay there on his back unconscious, the helicopter waving it like a retreat flag. And everyone laughed, the medics, the pilots, the eighteen-year-old me. That story worked on inmates. Hilarity. But I transitioned to something a little more civil, like how a phone could fit in a man's anus. No problem. For real. They are elastic. Anuses. It's the removing you have to worry about. And while that story might be, well, worse, or not, it was all I had. The change was sudden. It was the authority inside. It was the lack of it outside. One day a professor made fun of me for confusing "who" and "whom." The next I cuffed a serial rapist for trying to look tough at me. Anymore, I was only suitable on the inside. Anymore, sometimes I still am. It altered my genes. One big mass of outside and inside got mashed together, and the dominant strand won.

Y

THE drug-fueled kitchen-knife killer walked up. He was one of the jail-popular guys—good manners, talked Penn State football. He said, "May I please have an inmate request form?" I handed it to him. He said, "Thank you mightily."

And the day before, in the bucket on overtime, I fed one of the jail-bad guys. He received weekly visits from the goon squad and daily tickets from the bucket guards, and the schizo inmate next door to him told me, "Man, I don't mess with that nut." That jail-bad guy was in there with his water turned off to keep him from flooding the cell while working off his tiny one-year sentence for an intent-to-sell charge. A victimless crime.

When I got to his window he said, "Don't think I won't fuck you up because I don't know you."

Maybe because the kitchen-knife killer had a body, he didn't need to prove himself anymore. He was bad. We understood. So that let him be good (in jail). But I don't know. Maybe it was just because he was older. Age seems to slow men down. And jail seems to age men fast. He composed a polite letter to the unit manager wishing to address the shower situation on C side. The guys on A side kept trashing them at night.

A nineteen-year-old thief from dorm 1 yelled, "Ay, how 'bout a request form?"

I used the PA system to say, *Ay, how 'bout no.*

The man who once held a knife and stuck it into another human being said, "Lieutenant on the walk." Outside, a neck-bearded lieutenant stomped right through the marigolds. He stopped to give two inmates cigarettes. He patted them on the back and laughed hard about something.

He walked inside and avoided eye contact with me.

Hey, LT, what's good?

He didn't respond. Just signed the logbook and left.

I don't think I was jail-normal enough for him yet.

Next, an older guard with a gut walked in to use the bathroom. I had told him the week before that I didn't know the first thing about fishing. When he came out he said, "Hey, buddy, tell you what, come out to the house, we'll drink some beer and I'll show you how to clean some bass."

The nineteen-year-old thief walked up and said, "Hey, CO, my bad for yelling. How 'bout that request form now?"

The older guard said, "Beat it. We're out." Despite a stack of sixty of them sitting right there for the thief to see.

The thief said, "You guys be trippin'."

A fat sergeant with no criminal history walked in, filled a cup of coffee, and walked right back out. Not even a thank you.

I told him he could keep the cup.

He said, "You're fucking right I can, dick-lick."

After the door shut, the older guard said, "He's not like that on the street. He's actually a cool guy."

And I agreed. A real jail-cool guy.

A murderer named Lefty walked up. He had only one arm, his right. He poked me in the shoulder with his stump. It felt like a fist. He said, "I'm feeling generous. Today I'm making you honorary inmate."

He put his hat on my head.

It smelled like cigarettes and sweat.

It fit.

All I had to do was be the boss of two hundred good, bad men.

And smart enough to show up every day.

And dumb enough to show up every day.

Paper Clips

MELVIN ran up, stomped on my boot, then ran off. I had just shined them. But picture it: a kid darting around a park, peeking his head out from behind a slide, looking to see if he'll be chased. Hoping he will be. You pretend to look for this child while saying, Sarge, I don't see Melvin. Do you see him? And hearing Melvin's laugh. A belly laugh and a snort. Then a belly laugh because of the snort. Then a squeal. Then you pretend you can't see him creeping closer as quietly as he can while pressed against cell doors. Which isn't quiet. All those squeals. Then you round on him and yell, I'm going to get you! Which I did and gave chase past cold tables, up jail stairs, ducking iron grates, dodging a serial rapist, chasing giggles, snubbing a serious guard, following the giggles through the cage, down the stairs, a trash can knocked down, a gangbanger run over, more giggles, until I saw blood on the floor. Right inside a cell. Piles of it. And they were coagulating. I had never seen piles of blood before. Or since. They were dry on the outside, wet in the middle. The air smelled so coppery I thought my nose was bleeding. And a man lay in a bunk looking pale. He didn't move.

Melvin stood next to me. No more giggles.

I told him to go to his room.

He didn't move. I turned his shoulders for him and he walked off.

I radioed, *BC Desk, we got a guy cutting up!*

But I saw that the guy wasn't cutting up. Whatever he did, he was done. The action complete. I wasn't going in. Blood everywhere. I wore my scuffed boots home. So I kept my feet outside, held the doorframe with one hand, and swung in. I squeezed his shoulder.

The inmate opened his eyes and looked around like he was lost. I pulled him out of the bunk. He felt cold. He was middle-aged, short, white, and wearing only a T-shirt. I had never seen him before. Dried blood crusted the backs of his legs. Led all the way to his ass, which explained the piles on the floor. Some of it was shit.

Medical showed up. The inmate told the nurse, "I passed a razor from my rectum. It cut me." He said those words: "rectum" and "passed." Politically correct words for such a wrong act. He said, "I just transferred here."

I told him that he could buy razors at the commissary. Why smuggle?

He said, "Sorry."

The sergeant told me to take him to medical.

So I wrapped him in a sheet and took him to medical.

~

THE treatment building's ground floor was split between the doctor's office and observation area. The doctor half smelled like a hospital. The rooms standard: an examination table, roll stool, a sink in each. On the other half of the floor, through the heavy-duty security door, the infirmary, mental health unit, and observation area. No bars back there. Just doors and shouts and windows.

I walked through the security door and stepped over a stream of urine coming from the closest cell. The inmate in it shook his penis. Drops hit the window at my eye level.

He said, "You will respect me."

I saw five misconducts taped to his window. Writing another would be useless. I escorted Smuggler past.

A nurse told me to take him to get an X-ray.

So I took him.

The X-ray tech was pretty, which looked out of place in jail. She said, "Finally, I can start." Apparently she was waiting for a guard to show up and said something about state laws and escorts and procedures. She had three other guys scheduled. While the tech got the equipment up and running she asked me, "Are you married? Have kids? Any bad-boy habits?" I told her that I did Pilates and cross-stitch for fun. She laughed so hard I blushed.

The tech made Smuggler lie on the table. She told him not to move. I followed her behind the lead-lined wall. She smiled then pushed the button. "Security X-rays are exciting," she said. "You never know what you're going to find."

Smuggler was empty. No razors inside. No longer a risk to the institution. The doctor came in, looked at the X-ray, and, for some reason, told me, like I was responsible for him, "I'll do a colonoscopy to look for damage."

I said, Okay.

The tech asked me to get the next inmate.

So I took Smuggler to an observation cell and found Rodriguez, a little guy, five foot four or so. The first time I saw him he had big pom-pom pigtails. He came to the jail about a year after I started and had lots of friends immediately. "They're from the street," he told me in the yard. He grew up in Philadelphia. A day later, he beat up a much larger guy. Two body shots got the guy down low enough for Rodriguez to do some real damage. I hadn't seen him since. He was in the bucket the entire time. Inmates get ninety days for fighting, but he kept messing up inside. He fought with the guards over rules like not stepping to the back of the cell when his pancakes were delivered. Inmates always lost those fights. And the time added up.

Rodriguez wore an orange jumpsuit, the bucket's dress code. A bucket guard had seen Rodriguez with a lighter in his cell (contraband for bucket inmates). The goon squad searched his cell, twice, but couldn't find it. They thought, as Smuggler would say, it was in his rectum. So Rodriquez spent a week in an observation cell with the water turned off until we could recover it. But he went on a hunger strike. He told everyone, "No eating means no shitting."

The tech took me behind the wall after I cuffed Rodriguez to the table. The X-ray showed a full-sized lighter (the commissary only sold minis) sideways and down between his hips. The metal of it—the gear, the cap—was bright white compared to the shadow of its plastic. Also, the X-ray showed three wires in Rodriguez's abdomen: bright white crooked lines. He said, "Paper clips." He had straightened them out best he could and stuck them into his skin completely.

He said, "Sometimes they hurt."

The tech asked him, "Why do you do this?"

Rodriguez shrugged.

When I took Rodriguez back to his cell to continue his hunger strike, he said, "CO, let me get a smoke."

I told him, Good luck with that.

Next I picked up a tall kid. He said, "I heard a snap playing ball. My foot went sideways." Nothing was snapped on the X-ray. The next guy winced when he put his hand on the table. The X-ray showed normal. It seemed like he was there to see the tech.

She filed the new X-rays and, instead of locking the room and cutting off the lights like I expected, she closed the door. She walked behind the wall again and said, "Come look." And pulled out some X-rays. She stood close and held one up with two razor blades (thin ones taken from disposable razors) lit up. "Guess what this is a picture of," she said. It looked like a bowl of Salisbury steaks. I shrugged. "It's shit," she said. Then she showed me an X-ray of a bottle's shadow between somebody's hips. It was in his rectum. "It's a shampoo bottle," she said. "I can tell by the shape. He said that he sat on it by accident."

Right, I said.

The tech's shoulder was touching mine. We were alone behind the lead-lined wall behind a closed door. And in all my time working four-hundred-man blocks, and walking through six-hundred-man crowds out in yard to see what was happening in the middle (a fight), that was the first time I felt claustrophobic. She said, "Anything you put in your rectum should be tapered at both ends. Hypothetically of course."

Right, I said.

~

SMUGGLER'S colon was being examined when I left to work the lunch line: grilled cheese and tomato soup. It never tasted like soup, more like watered-down tomato sauce.

The guard working the exit door told me that he was at the hospital with the bottle inmate when it happened. The inmate, a sex offender in for raping a little girl, fainted while sitting on the toilet trying to remove it. He fell forward and broke his neck.

The guard said, "He's a paraplegic now. The spastic kind. A nurse strapped a spoon to his wrist so he could eat, but he just made a herky-jerky-mashed-potato mess."

He looked at me for a response. I had to say something a man over other men would say. Something offensive about the offender. Certainly emotionless.

I said, Weird. That was the best I could manage.

"Yep. And now everyone knows," He said. "He's a freak. His business is out there on Front Street."

Front Street is public knowledge. What is known about you. This book puts Rockview's business on Front Street.

Men came in and bitched about the grilled cheese. They were bricks as usual—you had to let them soak in the tomato water. I told them I didn't make it. Men chewed aggressively. The hall emptied.

~

MELVIN got me again. A huge stomp on my other boot the moment I walked through the door. I faked like I was going to chase. He ran off shrieking.

I didn't want to chase. And needed to sit. And I would never play tag with him again. Jail took the fun right out of it.

Out of everything.

The sergeant asked, "Too much today, Langston? Too much?"

Melvin peeked, belly-laughed, and snorted. He danced in the corner.

Too much.

A Timeline of a Condition

Three guards walked into a hospital. One had GonoherpasyphilAIDS. The other a gun. And the other, me, a Burst Appendix, which was great. I'd get to watch TV.

Burst Appendix, a guy down for murder in the second, lay shackled to the bed.

The guard I relieved said, "Hi and bye" and shut the door.

The hospital put jail types in the Infectious Disease Room. A suite, it had an outer room where the guard with the gun could hang out instead of sitting or standing in the hallway and hitting on nurses.

The policy was that the gun couldn't be in the room with the inmate so, naturally, Gun Guard stood right next to Murdering Burst Appendix watching TV. Murdering Burst Appendix looked at the revolver, then to his stapled incision, then lay his head back down.

If he went for the gun, I would bash him with my chair. That was the plan.

Gun Guard had time in. Sometimes it was easier to brace for the worst than reason with a guard who had time in.

Since we had two inmates in for repairs that day, policy required three guards. Gun Guard roved between the rooms. GonoherpasyphilAIDS and the ICU were on another floor. I couldn't wait for Gun Guard to rove.

Violent offenders were considered risks to public safety. So Murdering Burst Appendix was shootable if he tried to escape. But the other inmate downstairs—the repeat drug offender—wasn't. The rationale: he was less dangerous than a guard squeezing off 357-magnum rounds in a hospital. With him, well, we were just supposed to tackle him.

After an hour, GonoherpasyphilAIDS's guard called and said, "Herp-a-derp is good. But his mother, damn, she's been praying in Spanish since we got here. Wanna swap at lunch?"

Gun Guard walked to the door, patted the revolver handle, and said, "I'm taking my baby downstairs."

LIFE YEARS 3 TO 27

The hospital was ordinary: big, blocky, and beige.

I knew it well.

Every member of my family did time there.

Mother: a dozen surgeries.

Father: temporary blindness in one eye after catching a wiffleball line drive from my brother.

Sister: concussion after a bike crash.

Brother: born, then stitched up, then concussed, then stitched up, then concussed some more.

Me: stitched up also. The ER doctor said, "Finally, real medicine today. I'm tired of begging for stool samples." I had cut a two-inch zigzag into the meat of my hand with a box cutter while building a toilet-paper display at the grocery store.

JAIL YEAR 1.3

I wanted the gun.

The guard I relieved whispered only, "Shhhh, he's sleeping," like he guarded an infant.

Turns out the inmate had the surgery just minutes before I showed up—another burst appendix. His file: public risk, attempted murder.

The guard opened the door quietly. Stepped outside. Then slammed it shut with a jail-cell BANG.

Attempted Murdering Burst Appendix came to with a, "Uh!" Then he said, "I'll never smoke pot again." Then moaned. Then complained for the next hour about pain, commercials, hunger, and shackles.

The Gun Guard, another guy with time in, read magazines out in the foyer. I heard him snore for twenty minutes straight.

The surgeon came and did a good job ignoring me and the shackles. He talked to that Burst Appendix like a patient. "You should feel better," he said. "I sucked a lot of green and yellow out of you."

Lunch came: spinach, corn, and BBQ chicken.

JAIL YEAR 1.5

Another leaking, stapled, crooked path running up a guy's gut. Another burst appendix. I don't know what it meant that so many guys had the same problem. In America, one out of twenty thousand people need their appendix removed. But I guarded three in six months. And that was out of only two thousand inmates. That's one out of less than seven hundred. And according to my math, that makes something completely fucked: the food, maybe, or the water, or maybe some naturally occurring self-destructive acid found in shootable men.

The third burst appendix had "rapist" written in his file. A nurse walked into the room. She looked at his gut. She said, "That's one big incision."

Raping Burst Appendix said, "Can I get something to eat?"

The nurse said, "It's probably too early."

Raping Burst Appendix said, "Just bring me something to eat."

The nurse gave him crackers and left.

Raping Burst Appendix took one bite, then retched, then threw up into a pink container.

It had to hurt with that track in his gut. I asked, How'd those crackers work for you?

"Fuck you," Raping Burst Appendix said. "I'm not doing that again."

The nurse came back in and said, "How'd those crackers work for you?"

JAIL YEAR 1.7

I stuck my chest out around the civilians in the hospital waiting room. I had the gun. It was loaded. The civilians looked at us. I answered with my chest.

Hello, my chest said, this limping inmate in orange with the shackles and cuffs with me—yeah—the one about to get his ACL reattached—yeah—the one that the dozen of you elderly citizens are looking at—yeah—the one making you, the mother, hold close your two-year-old boy—yeah—that inmate, he is mine to shoot.

I thought: listen, everyone, I can squeeze off twelve shots in twenty seconds easy.

And: listen, everyone, that's even with reloading.

And: listen, everyone, relax, I got this.

LIFE YEAR 28 / JAIL YEAR 1.75

My wife shook me just before 2 a.m., four hours after clocking out of jail. I drove us to the emergency room.

In the ER, the bar-rush crowd roved around. Two young couples stood at the counter. One of the guys looked like he had gotten beat up. He bled from his mouth. His girlfriend looked at him in agony. I commiserated.

Two state troopers escorted a fifty-something lady, drunk or high or both, through the crowd. I saw and smelled that she had shit her pants. One of the cops was professional about it. The other laughed, pointed, and grimaced at her wet jeans. They took her down the hall for her blood test then jail sentence.

The woman who wheelchaired my wife up to the labor ward said, "Hi." Then after a pause said, "You don't remember me, do you? We used to work together."

I said, No, but okay, thanks.

I remember now that she worked with me at the water-bottling factory. For six months we worked back to back. I trained her to run the labeler.

My wife told her, "I think my water broke on your chair. Sorry."

Labor was hard. My wife sweat. We listened to classical music. She labor-breathed for hours. I went for a cup of coffee and walked by a Rockview guard talking to a nurse, his hand on the gun's grip. He didn't look at me.

My wife labored more. And when her blood pressure dropped real low at one point, I told myself to stop drinking so much. And then after ten hours of labor, my son was born with a soda-can-shaped head. "On account of the tight squeeze," our midwife said. "And his big head."

"Here," she said. "Cut the cord." It was tough, like a nylon rope.

LIFE YEAR 28 / JAIL YEAR 1.75 CONTINUED

Do you know what childbirth is?

Head trauma.

For the baby: physical—a squeezing, collapsing, and overlapping of skull plates.

For the mother: chemical—an oxytocin and lactocin surge to facilitate the bond, clot the blood, and begin the flow of milk.

For the father: mental—a visual and visceral experience of smells and noise accompanied by an emphatic link connecting directly and suddenly to a squeezed-headed being that you had only previously seen on a murky monitor.

I held him after the sink bath. He had a tiny cry and gray eyes.

Head trauma has been known to change people drastically. Makes some mean. Makes some nice. Others, just different.

LIFE / JAIL YEAR 0.1

I walked past the snack bar with Extreme Abdominal Distress. Inside the snack bar: eight tables, a grieving woman, and gentle music.

I was supposed to take Extreme Abdominal Distress to surgery, but ended up by recovery instead. After so many hospital trips, it was bound to happen: me losing my way.

The inmate: cuffed, shackled, in pain.

Me: armed, uniformed, and positioned for safety two steps behind a newer guard pushing the wheelchair.

I looked at our reflection in the windows of the snack bar.

When I was seventeen, I worked in that snack bar for community service. My sentence: 120 hours for criminal trespass and destruction of private property. Me and my friends had pulled a fence out of the ground at my junior high school's soccer field with my jeep. It was all in fun. Two Game Commission officers drove out of the nearby woods and blocked me in with their truck. They didn't think it was fun. They called the police. The police called my parents. The judge said I could do community service instead of paying the fines. I said, Thank you, and made milkshakes and malts and filled drink orders at the hospital for traumatized families and new fathers and that one sister who had an anorexic twin wandering the halls like a ghost.

With the inmate, it was a bad day to be lost. Extreme Abdominal Distress felt like an electrocution casualty when I helped him out of the van—that's how hot. He wasn't shootable. He was doing three years for criminal

trespass and destruction of private property. Same crimes as me. But he
was nineteen so received a felony conviction and jail time. My crimes wiped
from record.

The hallway was straight and bright and clean.

I asked him, What did you say your name was?

He grunted, "Brocklehurst. It hurts."

I said, we're almost there, Brocklehurst. Hang on.

The pistol was uncomfortable. It was heavy. I thought about my aver-
age-at-best shooting. I was my first time back at the hospital since my son
was born. I had gained weight. My son had napped on my chest for three
hours before shift. I watched out the window at a branch while he slept. No
TV. Just the branch. I didn't move. Then, feeling sluggish, I put my boots on,
drove to jail, clocked in, and checked the rounds in the pistol. It was angular,
cold, and sharp.

Coarse Grinds

WHEN the coffee machine went out in E block, the guards came together. First shift bought the new filters and a month's worth of coffee. Second shift, my shift, bought the new machine. And that was the most action we had in a nine-month stretch.

We broke it in on a rainy Friday. We clocked in at 2:00. Smolarski brewed. I made the first round and looked for damage and blood and gambling tickets. Football started that weekend.

Almost everyone was still on the block. Most slept. I walked back to the desk. The phone rang. The All Call told us what to say. We were middlemen. We got the ring and passed it on. We did this while pouring a cup of coffee. We did this without putting the sudoku puzzle down. We did this while estimating the probability of accidentally cutting the power cord on an electric hedge trimmer within the hedge trimmer's useful life—we guessed somewhere around 90 percent.

Smolarski made the announcement. "Yard canceled on account of lightning. Education line out."

An inmate down by the door said, "Blow me."

A few guys sat in front of the bay windows. There was no view. Only the old cannery. Men were once useful in that cannery. But that afternoon they just watched it rot.

Melvin walked by in an orange jumpsuit, his mouth open to the rain. He was bucket bound again. This time for exposing himself to his caseworker.

The bucket guard held his waist chain like a leash. Two inmates ran outside for GED classes. Melvin spat at them. The guard yanked the chain.

We were almost there, me and Melvin, to our time together in the bowels of the jail with restraints and ugliness.

Two inmates drug out the ficus trees to get the dust off. One of them, a lifer, said on his way back in, "Bored. Must. Find. Candy."

A tall and bald guy held out a scuffed plastic cup toward Smolarski. "Just a cup for this poor scofflaw?"

Smolarski said, "Scofflaw?"

"Scofflaw, you know, malefactor, convict, person guilty of a crime or offense? Call me 'con' for short." Then he said, "Too much Scrabble. Not enough coffee."

Most cons were addicts. Me too.

Scofflaw said, "I have a headache." It was the end of the month. Another week until pay and he needed to score. He was also a football analyst. In another life I could picture him on SportsCenter.

Four other cons stood at the desk. Friday was commissary makeup day. Scofflaw worked them hard for a coffee trade. "I have Milky Ways. I have a piece of Trident. I can guarantee the spread on six teams."

I said, hand over the gum. That was contraband.

He did and said something about being too old to want to escape and I stopped listening. Smolarski filled his own cup.

"Success," he said. "It's coffee."

The phone rang. The All Call tried to keep men moving with the chapel line. No takers. I poured a cup. I made a round. Every other bunk had a sleeping man. The rain came down hard. Windows leaked.

I opened the mop closet. A middle-aged con began mopping immediately. He was assigned to the paint shop. But it had been closed for three months. Union dispute. He aged five years.

I made another round with my cup. No one had moved. Cons slept with hats and boots on. I walked back to the desk. Scofflaw stood rubbing his scalp. His cup still empty.

My watch said 2:14. I had been in jail for fourteen minutes.

At least there would be mail to sort.

Then the mail officer dropped off the mailbag.

Then Smolarski made a copy of a sudoku he was stuck on so I could try.

Then the All Call rang. I picked it up. It started to say something but paused, then said, "Stand by."

So I stood by.

And sorted the mail at the side table. Cons streamed questions to Smolarski. I listened to his answers:

"When the All Call says so."

"Lightning, didn't you hear the announcement?"

"When the All Call says so."

"Don't you see him sorting the mail now?"

"When the All Call says so."

I organized the letters alphanumerically. Wrote up the list in my best handwriting. The con with the big head got his usual airmail from the Philippines. The pale inmate got his hunting magazine. The guy with the ears that stuck straight out got his used-car flyers. Jail keeps newspapers in business—the block got twenty a day. Word was that cons used it for armor in fights. They wrapped their bodies with it. But I never saw that. Not once. The papers talked about the same thing as the cons: football.

The phone rang. Smolarski beeped the PA. "Library closed, men."

A con from upstairs gave a loud "What?"

I finished the mail list. Took six minutes. I taped it to the wall. Inmates ran up to check. I used to make cons show ID cards, but by new-coffeepot Friday I knew all their names. In two minutes the mail was gone.

A few guys would be changing cells. That meant updating the count sheets.

But Smolarski handled that.

I made another round. I watched the storm. The ficus trees waved outside. There was a ring and a beep and the grounds crew was laid in (jail speak for work canceled).

A con said, "Damn."

Smolarski threw the filter and grounds in the trash. Scofflaw looked at them.

The storm blew. I worked my fantasy: grilling. That was it. I had zero aspirations except to experiment with paprika and onion powder on charred meat. I lived at jail speed, standstill. If I was off work, I walked my son around the neighborhood so my wife could concentrate on school. And I grilled. And walked around the neighborhood. And grilled.

Lightning flashed over the cannery. The lights flickered, which meant the air conditioning went out. I never noticed the hum of it until it was off. Cons looked at me. I told them I'd call maintenance once the storm passed. The breaker tripped with every light flicker. And we didn't have the keys for the fuse box.

The windows fogged up from 180 breathing and farting cons.

I did another minute watching clouds. They moved slow for a storm. I made a round. A guy down for third degree said he was going to take an hour-long shower. He had to practice his new song. Something about jail, no doubt. I went down to the staff bathroom and sat as long as I could. I worked on Smolarski's sudoku. My legs fell asleep.

I made a round. A thin guy paced. He ran for miles and miles out in the yard. Nobody could stay with him. He looked at the clouds. He worked in the wood shop. But the shop was closed. Yard was closed. He wrung his hands. He had a forty-year sentence.

The beep called for a man whose goatee touched his chest. Next for commissary. Only soft foods for him. He was on the waiting list for dentures, going on five months.

I did a round. It was 2:37. Only thirty-seven minutes in jail. I did another round when I was a minute older. I did a round after that.

Back at the desk Smolarski asked Scofflaw, "When you getting out?"

Scofflaw said, "Four to seven. When you retire?"

"Three to six."

Eight cons stood in line at the ice machine. When the block was full, the machine was empty.

I did a round. The humidity got bad. Smolarski propped open the door. Cards stuck to tables. Cons raised and called fantasy bets. Cons complained about the heat. Cons slapped dominoes. The ficus trees were probably going into shock with all that unprocessed atmosphere.

I picked up the ring and made a beep about how the storm was supposed to pass soon, maybe yard in ten minutes.

A con asked me if he could get a new mattress. I told him to catch me on a round.

A con asked, "Can I get an aspirin?" Not allowed.

Another, "Band-Aid?" Sure.

Another, "Shoelace?" Okay.

Another, "Pass to the yard?"

I asked him if he was kidding.

He said, "Naw. Just woke up."

I answered the ring. The All Call said, "Twenty minutes for yard." I didn't beep it. No point. A few guards mimicked the call in high voices on the line. Everyone could talk at once during the All Call. Somebody asked, "Who else is wearing purple panties?"

Three guys answered with "Me."

It was 2:50.

The Puerto Rican domino game got loud. Smolarski walked over and stood over the loudest malefactor. It got quiet. He came back and I made a round.

Then another.

The AC was out on my jeep. I thought about that while listening to the ice machine burn up. A con held his cup under the output. It dropped five or six tiny cubes every slow minute. The machine ground and ground. I didn't have the energy to correct him.

I wondered what number nap my son was on. Which dissertation chapter my wife was editing.

In one of the dorms an inmate watched a jail show. His hand in a bag of chips. Crumbs all over his bunk. The inmate on TV said jail is brutal.

Sure, I thought, if you edited out the three-month stretches when nothing happened.

I walked out and Scofflaw yelled, "Huzzah!" And stood arms raised. Then bowed. Then collected his Scrabble winnings. Looked like ten shots.

The loser spelled:

Y

O

F U C K

Their audience politely clapped and smiled.

And it was too hot for another cup. I used the bathroom. I made a round. I went home and grilled. Three months passed with no brutality. Someone said it was December. Melvin bobbed by. I watched a game of dominoes from the rail. There was a ring and beep. I made a round. Another three months passed. My son weighed sixteen pounds. Nothing new happened. I threw the filter and grounds in the trash. I made a round. Some guy in the shower sang, "Coulda been something. Coulda been some king." More heat and more steam. An inmate watched a show that showed an inmate watching a show. I made a round. Three more months passed. Melvin bobbed by. Melvin bobbed by. Nothing jail-new. My son said, "Ball." Ball! I stood at the rail. A con chewed gum. I let him. I avoided the desk. It wasn't even 3:00 yet and still raining hard. The wind died. No action brewed. Nothing. The clouds hung forever. Scofflaw had a full cup. Smolarski worked a sudoku. Twelve men stood looking outside, barely moving.

And I now know that saw it: the brutality of jail.

I made a round.

Trolls

FIRST TROLL

"Fa la la la la, la fucking la," sang the jolly guard.

We made a footpath through the snow while carrying trash bags full of inmate presents.

Over frozen cigarette butts we went.

Through the joint's icicle-covered concrete we stepped.

"Troll the ancient Yuletide carol!" he sang.

"Troll" means to sing something in the manner of a round, like how "Row, row, row your boat" is sung with two or more people—staggered and looping and constant. Incidentally, this is also how you run a jail: round after round after round. Everyone taking turns.

Trolls are also mythical creatures, usually ugly.

We guards trolled.

Jolly Guard kept looking at me to join in. Like it was expected. I adjusted the bags and told him I didn't know the words. He looked disappointed. He shrugged. He asked, "Don we now our gay apparel?"

My hat itched. But my hands were full. Trash bags over both shoulders.

Jolly kicked snow at two cats making their own trail.

Ten minutes earlier, he joyfully sang about penises from across the dinner table: "Why you biting that banana? Go ahead and throat it how you like. Glub, glub, glub." He smacked his butter knife on his lips.

Inside the trash bags were brown paper bags called holiday bags. Every inmate got one Christmas Eve. The kitchen staff packed them from the approved list of items:

Ball Point Pen, Standard, Black	1 ea.
Kellogg's Cereal, Single Serve Bowl Asst.	2 ea.
Nissin, Top Ramen Asst.	2 ea.
Frito-Lay, Individual Bag Asst.	1 ea.
Hard Candy, Individually Wrapped, Asst.	5 ea.
Toothpaste, Travel Size	1 ea.
Floss, Travel Size	1 ea.
Plastic Cup, 16 oz., Semi-Transparent	1 ea.

The evening meal was noodles with some kind of tan gravy. That's how it went on Christmas Eve: garbage before the feast. That's why I ate the banana.

Glub.

On Christmas, the jail cooked up real turkeys, real potatoes, instant stuffing, instant gravy, no cranberry sauce, and real pumpkin pie (square-cut from industrial sheets, but still good).

Oldheads got all the holiday vacation slots. So that left us, the youngsters, most under thirty, to distribute the holiday cheer. The lone oldhead working my first troll sat us down and said, "Years ago, this fucking inmate stole a turkey. It was twenty pounds and raw."

We young guards gasped.

"He plastic wrapped it to his body. Used damn near the whole roll."

We young guards laughed.

"He spent the entire day roasting it in his toilet. Stuffing and all. And not the instant kind. Bread and eggs and onions and spices. Everything. Ran the stinger right into the bowl. Flipped it every hour. Covered it with towels to hold in the steam."

We young guards nodded.

"Friends," the oldhead said. "That guy had about twenty friends that night."

I left story time and walked through the kitchen gate to get the holidays bags. Jolly came with. He smelled like inmate soap because he stole a bar every week to use at home.

By the pots-and-pans room, an inmate vomited into a trash can.

"Fa la la la," Jolly Guard said.

A blue shirt (jail speak for kitchen staff member) made me sign for 478 holiday bags. One for each of A block's inmates. Ten trash bags' worth. I picked up five. Jolly the rest. On the way out, the inmate who had been puking just minutes earlier stuffed noodles by the handful into his mouth from a tray in the hallway.

The snow crunched. Inmates left the treatment building two at a time. It was the end of visiting hours with its three-dollar, stressed-out, locked-in Polaroids. Inmates exited the chapel, smiling and hugging, feeling the spirit. They strolled around drunkish. A shot of real grape juice for communion was a treat.

Jolly Guard kicked on A block's door. "Ho, ho, ho!"

We threw the bags on the bubble's counter next to a red poinsettia. Every block got one. And every block let it die. Then we did nothing. We made no rounds. Showers were done. No yard after dark. Two inmates shoveled the walks outside the door (plastic shovels). Anytime I heard the scraping stop I checked on them. They went slow on purpose, smoking cigarettes, catching snowflakes.

We young guards played spades, hearts, and Yahtzee. We were mad about working. But that's okay. It was jail.

The previously perfect Christmas tree Frank and Sean decorated had been defaced with banana peels and candy wrappers. But its tinsel still radiated a glimmer of something: brown mostly.

No lieutenants or captains trolled. It was slow. At least Christmas had the good food. But the night before, all through the joint, it was depressing. Inmates fought over the phones. Two guards stood there to keep peace. We gave them fifteen-minute turns. That way everyone had an opportunity. They expected it.

We didn't troll the block. But other blocks trolled us. The phone rang and rang. The young sergeant fill-in made me answer. And each time this is how the conversation went:

A block, Langston speaking.

"Is Jolly there?"

Yes, I said. Hang on.

"No, I don't want to talk to him, I'm just checking for assholes."

Then they hung up.

The young sergeant rang the bell and sent the inmates to bed.

All the guards worked together to count and deliver the bags:

> 1 ea.

I took the top range. Ninety-one bags. Ninety-one inmates all accounted for. No inmates refused it. Most said nothing. Some played like they didn't want them. But took them anyway. I said nothing more than, Here you go. One skinny kid was alone in his cell, lying on his back and masturbating. Usually, right after count, inmates had some privacy. I threw his bag through the bars. He yelled, "Damn!" Next door, two guys had made stockings from newspapers and hung them above their toilet. Most guys had Christmas cards taped next to their bunks. I saw wreaths, reindeer, and women wearing bikinis and stocking caps. Some inmates said, "Merry Christmas." I said it back.

Back in the bubble, Jolly built a mousetrap from a wooden box holding inmate paperwork and ten inmate shoelaces. He used the doorstop to prop up the box—it probably weighed fifteen pounds. The bait: peanut butter on crackers. Mice squeezed through a crack at the bottom of the cage's steps, nibbled the crackers, and Jolly pulled the laces. These were mice, not rats, so they crushed easy and flat.

He stacked them. He cheered. He asked, "Hungry?" to whoever was closest when he picked up a fresh kill.

After six, no more came out. And the block was quiet. Nothing stirred. Except that skinny kid furiously beating off upstairs.

SECOND TROLL

A year and a half in jail doesn't earn a guard Christmas off. I spent my second Eve trolling the Mental Health Unit. The guard with me was a guy who, at the academy, put his testicles on a pool table to distract the shooter. He turned the TV on for the inmates: *A Christmas Story*.

We didn't need to shower the inmates. No mail to deliver. Definitely no yard. No program activities at all that day. Mental health staffers took their holidays at home.

The meals showed up: chicken patties—it could have been worse.

A Santa guard dropped off six holiday bags.

Testicles gave out the meals. Only one inmate refused, sort of. He was asleep.

The inmates/patients were all young. I watched their monitors. One drummed the door. One stood at his slit-of-a-window talking. No snow outside, just a dark gray sky. The sleeper lay cocooned in his blanket. The next flushed his toilet over and over with his foot. His neighbor, a failed suicide, with bandaged wrists, leaned on his door and watched the TV. So did Melvin. He stood on his tippy toes. Testicles made him laugh.

The phone rang.

"Is Langston there?"

Speaking, what's up?

"Nothing, just checking for assholes. Merry Christmas, asshole."

Click.

I buzzed Testicles back through the door. Then walked back to relieve the guard working the observation and infirmary areas. Infirm inmates quietly watched TV. Observation inmates, chemically unaligned, threatened suicide. I trolled. Two of the cells didn't have cameras. One guy was under his bunk sleeping. The other sat on his bunk. He wore a cast on his right forearm and hand. He chewed on it.

Five days earlier, he had chewed off the entire first joint of his index finger, bone and all. He bit it off, piece by piece. He was in jail for murder. He shot a man. But he claimed that his trigger finger did it by itself. It was possessed. The cast was meant to slow him down. He spit a piece of the cast onto the floor. No nub exposed yet.

His cell was dry. The water turned off so he couldn't soak the cast in his toilet. So he sucked on it instead. And bit it. And picked at it with his left hand. He did that until the nurse came through with a heavy dose of "Stop it." That was his present: a chemically altered state. He went to sleep with his knees on the ground, his face and torso on the bunk.

The guard for the area came back and poured Pepsi in the poinsettia. I walked back into the MHU. The phone rang.

"Is Testicles there?"

Yep, hang on.

"Don't bother, just checking for assholes."

Click.

Testicles buzzed me through the door to collect dinner trash. I brought their presents with me: holiday bags minus the cups and pens and toothpaste and floss—any weapons of self-destruction. We put that stuff in the closet for them until they could, maybe, in the future, graduate the pro-gram—which meant, congratulations, go back to regular jail.

I keyed the drummer's slot and traded his half-empty bag for his empty Styrofoam plates and cups.

The window talker told me, "Looks like a hurricane is coming." We made the exchange.

The sleeper raised his head when I dropped the bag to his floor.

The Toilet Flusher was on the floor. I kicked on his door twice. The only thing that moved on him was his chest. The nurse had got to him too. His trash was on his bunk. I pushed his bag through the slot.

The failed suicide said, "Thank you, sir."

I asked Melvin if he was good.

He said, "Why wouldn't I be?" I looked at his bare cell. He said, "Why wouldn't I be? Why wouldn't I be? WHY WOULDN'T I MOTHERFUCK-ING BE?"

I handed him his bag and retreated. He threw it across his cell.

What do you get for a guy who has nothing?

I turned and saw Testicles on the phone. With his other hand he buzzed me through the door. "Phone's for you," he said.

I answered. It was Jolly.

"I'm home," he said. "Not in jail. Like you. Fa la la, fucker."

Click.

A few days later, Finger Chewer got the whole thing off—all the way down to the knuckle. The regular guard in there said, "You should have seen him. He was happy. Happy as a kid on Christmas morning."

THIRD TROLL

I rounded the low-security, going-home block (E) every half hour. White poinsettia dehydrating on the counter.

Inmates left happy for visits and came back less than an hour later, frus-trated and bitching about the ice machine.

My partner answered the prank calls and watched TV. Smolarski was at home. He had time in. I organized mail—all those Christmas cards, their envelopes perfumed and nasty with lipstick. I stacked the eight packages that came on the floor behind the table. That kept those jail-approved gifts from a jail-approved catalog safe until they made it to the right inmate.

I wrote the mail list as fast as I could.

A tall, skinny black kid stood over me. "I'm trying to make the store," he said.

I told him to wait until I was done.

He said, "I'm trying to make the store."

I sent him to his dorm.

He yelled, "I can't wait no more!" on his way up the stairs.

I waited until he walked through his door to stand and tape the list to the wall. Then I trolled. I did. I trolled the block. The dorms emptied out on my way in. Most went for the list. Others ducked out the back door. Those were the trespassers.

"You're sick," the tall, skinny inmate said to me. "Sick. You got obsessive-compulsive disorder. This is your tic. Rounding on us like this."

I handed him a commissary pass. He smiled and said, "Just kidding, CO. Respect." And ran off the block.

I left for dinner. I expected garbage. And was rewarded: meatloaf, heavy on the onions. I ate industrial crackers, peanut butter, and canned peaches. Three guards sat at the guard table. We were short again. I didn't recognize them. All trainees. The children of the young bucks. They checked their watches obsessively.

In the kitchen, I signed for the holiday bags: 198 of them. And used a kitchen cart to roll them back to E.

It was clear and cold that Eve. And smelled like meatloaf.

Skinny and Tall stood at the ice machine. "This motherfucker isn't working. What's the point of having it if it never works?"

Automated disappointment.

I asked why would today be any different?

A group or Puerto Ricans got loud playing dominoes. Two guys yell-fought over the one good shower on A side.

Count time came and I called them down to collect their bags. They picked them up orderly and quietly. The ice machine clinked a few times, a miracle. Three extra bags lay on the cart. I put them in the closet behind the desk. I would use them later as rewards for shoveling volunteers. If it ever snowed, which didn't seem likely. My partner said, "It's supposed to snow on Christmas." He was young. Younger than me.

Outside, nothing but jail lights. What a disappointment.

Tall and Skinny walked by. "Snow on Christmas, cakes on birthdays, blowjobs on anniversaries. That's how it's supposed to work."

Next morning, I conditioned my son for future holidays. His first Christmas. His first presents. Just two: a plush lion and a ninja guy. He played with the wrapping paper and cried when he bumped his mouth on the floor—it was like he didn't know it was Christmas.

After lunch at home, grilled cheese, on that third troll, I drove back to Rockview. Ate a proper and decent Christmas dinner. Had seconds of the pie. Watched *A Christmas Story*. Laughed a few times with inmates. Answered prank calls. Trolled. Some jail-goods decorated one of the ficus trees with shoelaces and chips bags. An inmate said into the phone, "Stretch. Because when I get home, I'm going balls deep." Two guys fought about the ice machine. One had emptied it for a slushy. I said, Behave. Then trolled more. But didn't write anyone up. It was Christmas after all, wrapped up all nice and nasty.

Grace

CAPTAIN "Grace" was built like the perimeter patrol truck: six foot three with a large hood—that was his gut—and you just knew he got shit for gas mileage. When he walked, he rocked. The rocking came from him constantly adjusting his belt and pants.

I looked at Grace like he was a curiosity. Here was this thing. A relic. I got the same feeling looking at Grace as I did looking down the musty stairs to the original bucket. It was in the basement of the main bunker. No one went down there anymore, where men were fed with buckets and pissed and shit in others. No running water, just punishment. I stood up so Grace could sit down when his rounds brought him through E block's door on a warm evening in June. He took his hat off and ran his fingers through his white curls—thin on top, and a bit too long for regulation—and cleaned his glasses on his tie.

Grace, that goon, used to beat inmates unconscious.

Sometimes he used a baton. "I smashed one inmate so hard," Grace told me. "That he reverted back into a child. He pissed his pants. He cried for his mommy. He had to be transferred out."

I don't know why he told me stories like that. And few inmates came up to the desk while he was there—all of a sudden they had all the Band-Aids they needed. Only the lifers stopped by. One of them, Toms, a small man, approached. "Grace here," he said. "Is a living, breathing legend."

Twenty-five years earlier, the inmates in the bucket, while Grace operated on the goon squad, knew the ease with which he beat them. They felt how he got full extension with his strikes, despite the confined space. How he did it gracefully, without a hitch, with a smooth and solid drumming, that earned him his name.

Word is it was beautiful.

"You come over the top," Grace said. "And don't stop."

Grace was one of those guys who, even at fifty-four, could still put up 350 pounds on the bench. He powerlifted and used to compete.

But anything over fifty in jail is old—for both guards and inmates. Guards usually retire by then. And inmates usually mature out of their life of crime and leave, or die. Incidentally, fifty is also when a man's testosterone level rides down that hill, that steady decline to the flatline. You're still a man, just different.

Toms knew that just watching Grace exercise his heavy hand was risky. Once while Grace was disciplining an inmate, he caught a lieutenant standing behind him in the forehead with one of the back swings. The lieutenant retreated from the cell with a three-inch lump swelling up fast above his eye.

That was just one indirect and accidental blow from Grace. Imagine an intentional one. A well-targeted crack. Solid contact between the skull and the baton's sweet spot—that's the spot two inches from the end where the impact won't sting your hands. "Bones," Grace said. "Hurt more than hitting baseballs wrong."

But Grace's hands-on days were long finished by time I met him. I was hired in the era of cameras and lawsuits. Not once did I even see a baton inside the fence. And the general rule for current bucket jobs was that they came with the expectation of court dates. Work the bucket long enough and you will be named in a lawsuit. "Don't worry," Grace said. "You get paid to take the stand. It's a paid day off. Extra for lunch." Most lawsuits came from cell extractions, inmates claiming abuse at the hands of the goon squad—even though all cell extractions were videotaped. But there were also, occasionally, constitutional lawsuits. Some general denial of rights for inmates, like only receiving three-quarters of an ounce of cheese on taco day instead of the prescribed full ounce.

Grace said, "Legend no more, Toms. I'm retiring next month."

Toms said, "It won't be the same."

Grace said, "It's not the same anyway."

Toms was one of the two hundred inmates at Rockview serving the other death sentence: life. A life sentence in Pennsylvania means life. There is no parole. Toms had been in jail since he was fifteen. He shot his also-fifteen-year-old girlfriend three times with a shotgun at close range. But she didn't die. So he put her in a creek. It was winter. She floated. So he slid her under the ice. The cause of death was drowning, officially. Unofficially, in his pardon application, it was Toms's mother dying from cancer when he was ten years old, his thirteen brothers and sisters scattered in foster homes, his speech impediment, his fear of leaving his fourth foster home in five years, his pump-action shotgun that he had access to and was trained to fire fast with, and his girlfriend's lie that he had made her pregnant that did her, and him, in.

Grace said after Toms left the desk, "At least he won't die a virgin."

Toms was maybe five foot six and about 140 pounds. On my way to the block that afternoon, I walked by him building a new strip-search shack for the main gate. He hung out the doorframe and nailed on the roof with a nail gun, firing fast. He smiled and waved the gun at me.

He had been in the wood shop for some time. He helped transform the death room into the guard's training room, artistically trimming the room in oak. He built the bench-press benches out the yard, the racks in the block's laundry and sheet rooms, the podium in chapel, the pegboards for hanging my hat in the closet in E block, the everything. He built everything, and he built it to last. Proof was in the paint, all the layers on all that wood. And Toms himself was brown and creased and bent, a jail-old fifty-three. Which put him at thirty-eight years in prison—no virgin at all.

But it was probably youth, that most unstable of states of mind, that did him and his girlfriend in. Today, juveniles are judged as "delinquent" rather than "guilty." Sentencing for juveniles operates with the belief that their behavior is malleable. Rehabilitation and treatment are considered goals.

Adult behavior is believed to be static, and the sentencing aims to make the punishment proportional to the offense. So only men are found guilty. And men are only considered men when they reach the "age of majority" (law speak for adulthood). That's when minors are no longer minors and they get to assume control over their persons, actions, and decisions. They can do awesome things all of a sudden, like vote and enter binding contracts. When I hit the age of majority, I joined the army and bought—on credit—an overpriced and unreliable truck that I sunk all of my army pay into. Then got a bad tattoo. Then a high-rate credit card. Then an over-priced computer with that high-rate credit card.

Thanks a lot, age of majority.

The age of majority is typically eighteen, which, for men, is also when our testosterone is at its highest—and that just seems dangerous.

Toms walked by the desk and stepped outside to smoke. He did that a lot. Grace told me that the Pardons Board had denied Toms a pardon. "Everyone thought he was going to get it," Grace said. "One of the mainte-nance guys was even going to give him a place to stay and a plumbing job." The father of Toms's victim had forgiven him. Toms has a picture of them hugging each other in the visiting room.

But his pardon was denied because of another Rockview lifer.

"Freeman was our most famous inmate," Grace said.

Freeman murdered an elderly woman when he was sixteen. Got life. But he applied for a pardon seven times during his twenty-five stretch and was granted one in 1994. He left Rockview with his haircutting and tree-surgery certificates to murder three more people and rape another two. He did these crimes within ninety days of his release.

Grace said, "He worked out in the greenhouse, minimum security."

At his new trial, Freeman said, "Over twenty-five years I spent in some of your worsest prisons that a penologist can conjure up in his twisted men-tality and then you let me out of your prison."

Grace said, "Nobody talked to Freeman. He was an asshole. That's why he worked with the plants. But the board didn't ask any guards about him."

The pardons board voted four to one to release him. The lone dissenter thought Freeman was too young at forty-one to be trusted not to revert to crime. Today the board must have a unanimous vote. Toms's vote was four to one when he was denied.

Toms came back inside the block and said, "Freeman made it hard for us."

Only eight lifers in Pennsylvania have been pardoned in the twenty years since Freeman. Nine were pardoned in the two years before his re-lease. Toms would find no forgiveness from the state.

Toms jumped on the back of a passing inmate and said, "Giddyup."

Grace cleaned his glasses again then tapped his radio hard on the counter. He stood, adjusted his belt, put his hat on, and said, "Langston, keep 'em in line," then rocked out the door. As soon as the door shut all the inmates came up to the desk again and crowded me with all their needs for cell-change paperwork and shoelaces and passes to the library and didn't I know that the laundry-room door was supposed to be unlocked three minutes ago?

~

THE pardons application asks, "What efforts have you made to rehabilitate and improve yourself?"

Grace, Toms, and Freeman all did time together at Rockview. They were all close to the same age. They knew each other. Grace built his reputation with his legendary swings. Freeman grew and nurtured something out in the greenhouse. Toms transformed the buildings of Rockview.

Grace needed no pardon—he retired free and clear. Freeman received his pardon, then another life sentence, this time in New York. And Toms was refused until the Supreme Court ruled to allow juvenile offenders serving life sentences (about twenty-five hundred nationally) a chance at parole. Toms finally left Rockview in 2016.

~

A WEEK later there was a staff assault on CB block. An inmate took a swing at a young sergeant. The inmate missed. But the sergeant still radioed, "CB block here, send help!" And he got it. Nine guards responded.

Grace, breathing heavy, pulling up his pants, adjusting his radio, showed up at the end of it . . . at the end of ten young and energetic guards on top of that inmate, one choking him, two on each arm, two on each leg, another kneeing him in the gut, and the first thing Grace said, that king goon, that destroyer of men, that rocking truck of a man, that living legend, was, "Don't hurt him! Don't hurt him!"

American Cockroaches

I WOKE up and my wife said, "You were grinding your teeth again." Then I drove to jail and ran through a cloud of 2-chlorobenzalmalononitrile (chemistry speak for teargas) to get to E block.

Teargas smells like a mix between exploded fireworks and uppercuts. Depending on the dose, it can stop breathing, produce six-inch-snot ropes, induce vomiting, or cause miscarriages. The guard running with me gagged about his sinuses. He claimed he once slit a deer's throat to save ammo. He was tough like that.

That day the lung constriction was light, carried by variable winds with the expectation of rain and intermittent nasal discharge. But I felt a lawsuit brewing. And found fifty inmates standing inside the door complaining about the vast oppression of their lives because they lived in a jail and yard was delayed. Turns out the goon squad had set off a cache of expired teargas canisters over at the jail shooting range. High winds blew the cloud over the compound.

My hair was going full-on salt and pepper.

I closed the door and a muscle freak stepped to me and said, "You can't be keeping me in here. I need my yard. I'm a spring. You know springs weigh more when compressed, right?"

A crowd of inmates stood behind him.

The crowd said, "Power tripping again."

The muscle freak said, "That's physics, CO."

The crowd said, "Drunk on that shit."

The muscle freak said, "That's Einstein. The science of stress."

The crowd said, "Let us out."

Ammo Guard ran to the bathroom.

One of the morning shift guards said, "They slept all morning. Not a peep." Then walked off the block. His partner followed. I locked the door. They covered their faces with their shirts and ran through the chemicals. You couldn't see the teargas. Normal gray out there.

The phone rang. Inmates ran for the door and piled up against it expecting yard out. The All Call said, "Count clear. Yard delayed. Blockout authorized."

The twenty extra pounds on me looked like thirty-five. That's what I saw in the laundry-room window across from the desk. That and a double chin.

The Einstein lover said, "Man, you just don't know."

The rest pinched their faces like they smelled something foul.

And I told them to take it in. I said it to the ones hand-printing the door. I said it to Einstein. I yelled it over the PA, *Take! It! In!* I didn't care about their precious lost yard or authorized blockout. I wanted them away from me.

I suffered from an acute overload of complaints.

They scattered.

I had found a white nose hair the day before. It hung long and heavy from my right nostril, embedded like a fence pole.

I made a round. Ammo Guard took over the desk. He held a wad of tissues to his nose. I hoped to catch somebody doing something. Anything. I wanted to take someone's parole. Hand out some bucket time. Gift a misconduct. Enjoy one less member of the oppressed crowd. Complaints always quieted down when one took a trip to the bucket.

The bathroom on A side stank. An inmate grunted away inside the stall with a sheet for a door. A block worker scrubbing a sink said, "Damn, man, hit that with water." The grunter flushed. I left.

The PA beeped and Ammo Guard let the inmates out to the yard. The All Call had called all clear.

I watched from the second-floor rail.

Inmates ran by. The door slammed with every oppressed inmate. The spring was sprung. Maintenance replaced it every six months. Doors take a beating in jail. Inmates drug chairs around blockout. Floors take a beating in jail. Inmates snapped their shirts dry after showers. Shirts take a beating in jail. Inmates paddled together their shower shoes, drug their feet, burped loud, table-whacked, and coughed up phlegm. Ears take a beating in jail. Eight inmates stopped at the desk with hands on hips and loud voices. Ammo Guard handed out grievance forms. Guards take a beating in jail. I stomped on a cockroach that sprinted out from under the door behind me and ground it into the linoleum. It was two inches long. Had useless wings. An inmate walked by and said, "They talk shit."

I said, What?

"That's how they communicate, cockroaches, through chemicals in their shit."

I said, Who knew.

"That was an American cockroach. By the way." He walked to the desk. That's where all the inmates were. They ran Ammo Guard, asking for laundry, for request forms, for cell-change paperwork, and cried if he said no.

Another cockroach scuttled by. I opened the door where it came from. On the bolted-to-the-floor desk sat a TV, one of the clear ones. But the inside looked coated with leaves. Until I hit the light. The leaves picked up and blew. They were roaches. They gathered in the corners. I ran to the laundry room, grabbed a sheet, ran back, and stuffed it in the crack under the door. What I wanted was five gallons of gas and a lighter.

Some days my lower back didn't let me stand straight up—that was one of them. Other days my upper back didn't let me turn my head to the right.

Inmates moved to E block so they could roam free at night with no locks. I heard the white kid in one of the corner cells took on all comers for sex. His door was open. I heard about a cell phone on the block. I opened the exit signs, determined to find it. I knew we had the best tattoo artist in the jail. I confiscated a bucket from his cell that he had somehow gotten from the supply closet. Probably used it for a stool.

A guard dropped the mail off. I walked down and threw it in the back room. I usually did the mail right away for all to see. But not on teargas-bull-shit Saturday. The bag was visible through the door. Inmates looked at it, rubbing their hands together, congregating around the ice machine, trading sugar packs and creamer, talking.

I made coffee. Ammo Guard went for a round. I was stuck.

Einstein came down and asked for a pass to the yard. Of course he missed it. Why would he be responsible and listen to the announcement?

No, I said.

"No?"

Yeah, no. You missed it.

"I missed it?"

Good, so you heard me.

"I heard you?"

Is there an echo in here?

"Echo?"

Everything he repeated was an octave higher. His eyebrows raised. He was a thief who preyed on the elderly. And he actually thought I was there to serve him.

The coffee was done. I looked at myself in the laundry-room window again. I needed a haircut. I needed a shave.

"I need a yard pass."

Sure thing, I said. Anything you want. You earned it.

Jail speak for no.

"You think you can deny my yard?" His voice squeaky then. His eyes wide open.

Oh, it's mad.

That was my thought: It is so mad.

Good.

I regretted learning names. I shouldn't have looked at files. Jail worked better when they weren't people.

I said, You missed your chance.

The inmate stood there.

It stood there.

I was such a professional guard until that moment. My job was not to judge, only to correct. Sure, I stole boots and other things, like a winter jacket on the coldest day of the year, that's how I maintained control. They forced me, those criminals. It was their fault I thought. Totally their fault. I was one of the good ones. Didn't they know?

"So can I get a pass to the yard?"

No, and we're done.

It left.

But my attitude wouldn't.

~

NOBODY made me take that job. I could leave any time. This is something I began to obsess about. But I was making more money than I ever had. And I was no closer to a degree or valuable skill. The way of the blue collar is to stay in a uniform until a higher-paying one comes along.

My wife was on the job market, looking for her future, her degree almost in hand. We would make a decision soon: stay or go? But I had taken the sergeant's test the weekend before. Was waiting for the results. I could make more. So much more.

A lieutenant walked on the block to sign the logbook. He was a lifer, making seventy thousand a year. That's a blue-collar millionaire. One with only a high-school diploma. Why wouldn't he stay inside? Why wouldn't I?

Outside was the big ol' blue-collared underpaid world waiting to stomp people flat.

~

EINSTEIN walked back to the desk.

"Sorry," he said.

I wanted to let Einstein know that we were not the same. That he was less. That he forfeited his rights when he cashed his neighbor's social security check. That the birthday candle I had seen him light a few weeks earlier—a burning can of boot polish—I was glad for that. Happy birthday. And many more.

Exactly like that one.

My response: Take it in.

Jail speak for fuck you.

He stared. I stared. He said, "I'm only going in because I don't want any trouble."

The phone rang. The All Call. Chapel line. I announced it over the PA.

He stood there.

"I don't want any trouble. You're looking at a real OG. Ask my squad."

I wondered if by squad he meant his rapist celly.

He intruded on my already beat day. I got no sleep, had a garbage break-fast, had no time to take a dump or shower because I was on sick-baby duty until thirty seconds before driving into riot gas and verbal combat.

But all this is just me being angry. Please excuse all this crying. I could quit at any time. Pay the rent with my high school diploma and honorable discharge. Get a factory job to not even break even. Or the GI Bill would pay me $586 a month to go to school if I wanted. Five hundred and eighty-six dollars! Imagine it. Thank you, army, for getting me to sign that deal. That's American dream stuff. All of life's advantages right there at $586 a month—minus tuition, books, food, rent, car insurance, and life and life and life. Solid deal.

I told Einstein, Yes, I'll have to do that, ask your squad.

I couldn't understand the entitlement. I wanted restraint. Like me: the paradigm of patience and understanding (ignore the eyebrow twitch, the sneer, the grumbling from my teeth).

I had committed to the idea that I did not have a talent for the job. I was playing a role that I could not maintain. But for the blue-collar millionaire life, I had to try.

My lungs constricted. My eyes burned. I looked at Einstein.

Take it in.

"You don't have a life, do you?"

You can't write a guy up for asking dickish questions. Especially true ones.

The week before I went to the dentist. He told me I had broken a tooth. A molar. Cracked right down the middle. He said it could split. So he pulled it out and gave me a week's worth of pain pills. I remembered no complaints from that week. No comments about yard or abuses of power. I remember nothing but a fog of medicated rounds.

It was a good week, the best in a year. Only cost a tooth.

Einstein's mouth opened and expelled something like, "This is jail, man."

The expulsion fell right on the desk and lay there, a pile of shit talk.

His mouth opened again. More expectorate fell out. "Why you playing?"

I saw a warped form moving its mouth.

Its mouth moved again. "This is jail."

Hit that with water, I said. More shit talk.

"What?"

I said, Hit that with water, then walked into the backroom, leaving the desk empty.

Chunks of Ugly

I.

Melvin was a crack baby. This isn't an insult. He really was a crack baby. His mother used crack daily. And inside her he was altered, addicted. That Freudian saying about how men spend their entire lives trying to get back in the womb—imagine how he felt.

I looked through the window of Melvin's cell. It was an observation cell. I, in my state-issued prison guard uniform, looked baggy and cheap. I had those official-looking patches on my shoulders. Short sleeves meant summer. The black pants were wrong. The crotch was closer to the knees than to the crotch. Above the washing directions, the tags read, "Made by Inmate Labor."

Every jail labored the inmates. This one used to have a cannery, leather shop, and butcher shop. Big House Industries, that was the brand name. Inmates packed beans and corn into industrial-sized cans. They made belts and purses. And they used to eat the cows. But the cows were only for show when I rattled the gate behind me. They were there so the state didn't take the jail's land—use it or lose it. Plus they gave the inmates something to do. A guard took a few low-risk inmates every day down to shovel out the barn and serve up inmate-grown hay. The cows, though, they didn't do anything. Hauling themselves to the trough was the only exercise they got. Once they escaped, but stood outside the fence, waiting, I guess, for dinner.

Melvin was strapped down flat on his back. He, in his state-issued, suicide-resistant smock, looked sick and cold. The smock was a sack, gold color. Holes cut for his head and arms—triple stitched for strength. He was immobilized. Five-point restraints, it's called. Number four on the use of force continuum. It falls before lethal force and right after the use of chemical munitions. This was his correction for breaking a rule. He painted his cell with his shit. And this was it for Melvin. This was as good as it was going to get. At least there he got some attention.

From birth, Melvin was taken into state custody and placed—more like deposited—in foster homes for his entire life. He was raised—more like stored—in these homes until he was old enough to go to jail. At twenty-one, he stood four feet six inches tall. He had the mentality of a five-year-old. An angry one. And this crack baby, this product of pollution, this three-year resident of a state correctional facility, was a convicted arsonist.

Inside Melvin's cell, no sheets or blankets. His comforts were his smock, his mattress, and the torso, leg, and arm straps attached to the bunk. Every few hours guards flipped him—it took six guards. Five to flip, one to videotape.

Those cells weren't just for the Melvins of the world. A week's worth of observation-cell vacation was only five whispered words away: "I'm going to hurt myself." It had a policy, the jail did, that required observation for anybody suicidal—fakers or not. Guys broke down in jail. Rape victims, guys who lost fights, and guys who came up hot for incurable STDs were all given timeouts—to rest—to be looked at every fifteen minutes. Those cells were for them. Except during football season. Then they were for the guys who couldn't pay their gambling debts. It was either suicide watch in a smock or the big guy with a lock in a sock because you owed him eight oatmeal cream pies. Temporary escape, that's what inmates called those cells.

Hour two into a sixteen-hour double shift, I relieved the oldhead guard working the area. He went for his breakfast. Since it was attached to the jail's infirmary, two nurses sat there. They had on those scrubs you see in real hospitals. There, though, they looked like lunch ladies.

Melvin had a reputation with the nurses. He spit, gesticulated, door-kicked, cursed—he did all the things boys do when they're mad, and more. He exposed himself. I wouldn't say they hated him, those nurses, but it was close to that. They looked at me like it was my fault he was in here with them.

His inmate number started with a D, which meant his sentence began when I started. Inmates with A numbers had been in jail since the Vietnam War—or longer. Respect, they said, was given to them for their low number. Somehow I'm not sure "respect" is the right word. But they had the best jobs. A life sentence got a guy a job in the staff dining hall, or chapel, or gym. No A numbers worked the pots-and-pans room. That room was hot, wet, and filthy—it was work.

I tucked in my shirt. It was so baggy I couldn't see my keys.

I asked, Melvin, you okay?

II.

It took three years wearing that shirt before I found myself looking through that glass at Melvin. First day this oldhead black guy suggested I say excuse me when I walked by him. He grit on me. I didn't know how to respond. An inmate had a seizure the next day—I held his head. He drooled on my hands. Everything was made of concrete and steel, and it was all falling apart. The jail fed its bucket agitators food loaves. The secret ingredient: every-fucking-thing. The cook ground together mashed potatoes, waffles, lima beans, Jell-O, oatmeal-raisin cookies, and grits. Used punishment to bind it—and an egg. My third week, I rounded a range and saw a copper wire taped in a crack in the wall. I found the end and pulled. Country music twanged in the distance. I followed the wire for twenty feet, removing it from the crack. The music got louder. The wire ran above three more cells then down into a fourth. I gave it a yank. An inmate's TV fell off the desk. The wire was his antenna. He couldn't afford cable. Or, probably, a new TV. I speed-walked away and didn't return to that cell for five hours. When I finally did, I saw that the TV still worked, the inmate watching a commercial through static. But it bothered me, my carelessness. I stepped on the biggest cockroach I'd ever seen. The guard with me said, "You need to wash your boot. If it was female, her eggs will hatch in your house." Too late. Jail already hatched there. Ask my wife. She listened to me beat the basement heavy bag until my knuckles split. I watched a cross-dressing inmate apply shoe polish as lipstick. A guard told me he could get me a monkey for fifty bucks. An inmate spit on his bars right where I was about to grab. I grit on him. I washed my hands. An oldhead mean-mugged the grit right out of me. I opened the exit sign on one block. Inside was a cassette tape from the chapel. The label read, *Salvation Blooms Waterless,* but when I played it at the desk, it was Run DMC. An inmate with a mullet walked by and said, "Reminds me of getting high and fucking." I turned off the radio. I washed my hands. I grabbed an inmate by the sleeve because he didn't show me his pass. He growled. I washed my hands. An inmate told me, "Everyone wants happiness. And everyone will fuck over anyone to get it." I was happy with my paycheck. I stood at roll call waiting for whichever job I had to beat, maybe a tower, a truck, a shower, a shack, a gate, an open expanse of torn-up grass. A temporary goon helped during a cell extraction. His job was to put a spit hood on the inmate. But he put it on himself instead. At two years in, nothing surprised me anymore. Some guard always farted on his radio. There was the rectal bleeding, the prepackaged sour-milk bombs, the skull fractures, the boredom. There were chumpies and joints and johns. An inmate didn't want the food loaf anymore. He threw feces at staff because of it. He covered his window with a blanket because of it. He got gassed and tackled and carried out of the cell because of it. In my free time, I watched car-accident videos because of it. I drank because of it. I sparred with everyone because of it. Brown uniforms run-walked to the yard as soon as the bell rang. Gray uniforms peeled off the browns for pat downs, ID checks, and threats. I turned keys. Inmates slept. Inmates self-improved. Inmates fought. Inmates wrecked. The brown uniform fits everyone, from the four-hundred-pounder to the fifty-four-incher. Nobody is harmless. Everyone I saw outside jail was an ex-con. The forty-year-old pushing carts at the supermarket: ex-con. The cashier handing change back to my birthday-rich son: Megan's Law ex-con. I inspected keyholes, food slots, anuses. When I looked at one inmate fully clothed, all I saw was the mole on his left ass cheek. Five white hairs grew from it like ghost fingers. I felt for my keys. An inmate told me I looked weak. I walked in his cell later and took his ID card and threw it in the trash. It would cost him ten dollars and two weeks of missed visits. I ached to tell him that I did it. But was too weak. A new guard walked through the gate—he spit, crotch-adjusted, swore, and blended right in. I fell asleep on night shift. I watched an inmate have a seizure and didn't want to touch him because I had no gloves. I couldn't believe it. I always had gloves. I saw authentic inmate boots for sale on eBay and thought jail. I checked my bank account and thought jail. I walked into a Salvation Army store, saw fifteen clear-plastic TVs, and thought jail. I listened to Johnny Cash's

"Folsom Prison Blues" recorded live at Folsom Prison and heard jail—not in the lyrics, but in the bell ringing at two minutes and twenty-three seconds in. A prison bell in the background. A count bell. A count time. Standing count. Lights on. I went to a coffee shop and an older guy said, "Hello" to me and smiled—and I thought, what's your motive? I picked up phones and checked them for boot polish because I knew guard humor. I discovered that asking, "Are you arguing with me?" makes everyone—inmates, wives—automatically say, "No." I washed my hands. I felt for my keys. An inmate told me, "No. I will not take down my kid's Christmas card. You guys bitch about every-fucking-thing." So when the range was empty, he at yard, I pulled his TV off his desk. Not really pulled it off. But picked it up and smashed it into the concrete as hard as I could. And that's how jail picks at you, a little for a lot. And I knew, right then, that sorry wouldn't fix it. I was guilty. Gone. The institution was not a dream, an ideal, or an opportunity. Control was an everything-loaf. Rockview was a grinder. And I was bound to it for money—only—and that does not work. I had to leave.

III.

That uniform worked me. It got dirty. Driving home with the windows down didn't get the jail off. I needed a shower to give my son a bath.

The jail was a holding tank. There might have been rehabilitation. But I didn't see it. I only saw separation, the good from the bad, if you can call the good good and the bad bad. Jail is for people like Melvin. Fifty-four inches of aggravation and frustration, he was the opposite of a celebrity. He was the guy no one cared about, missed, or loved. In three years, he never had a visit.

How Melvin got there was his entire life.

He looked up at me.

"CO," he said. "I feel sick." He said it in that breathy sick-speak that people do.

And he puked. He puked before I could process what he said. He didn't even turn his head. He just puked scrambled eggs all over his face. His dark complexion made the eggs look neon. I watched that little prepackaged criminal. He was choking on half-digested, state-issued eggs and sputtering for air. He didn't look like he was dying. But I had to help—just in case.

I felt nothing. No anxiety. No panic. I pulled out the stereotypically huge key ring with those stereotypically huge keys on it.

Melvin started crying. I heard him in there. He cried when he could get that short breath of air between heaves.

I opened his door. It was the kind with the metal slot guards used to put trays of food through or inmates used to throw urine out. The polluted air hit me, tangy and sour.

Stale and bitter nurse number one said, "You better wait for a lieutenant." Number two stared and did nothing. Bystander effect, I think it's called.

It had this rule, the jail did, that you needed a lieutenant as a witness when you had to touch an inmate. Because of lawsuits, it claimed. Most of the time, guards were wallflowers. We watched with our radios and whistles at the ready. Only the guards in movies carry guns and nightsticks inside the fence.

Melvin twisted under the straps. It was hard to work the oversized brass buckles with him panicking. He rolled to the floor on all fours the moment he was free. I stepped back then because the puke, it was splattering.

The nurses kept getting ass-time. The jobs where you sat all day were coveted. Tower jobs were the ultimate. The towers were for show—a show of force it's called, number one on the use of force continuum. And eight hours straight, the tower officers showed that force, sitting. The towers are eight feet by eight feet with their own toilets and spotlights. There was a rope in each. It was for lunch. The farm patrol officer, while driving inmates down to feed the cows, stopped to feed the towers. For the tower guards, hauling up those lunch coolers on the ropes was the only exercise they got. One oldhead guard with a pomade wave in his hair said, "It takes twenty years of seniority to get a tower. Fifteen if you're lucky." He got lucky, he said. Somehow I'm not sure lucky is the right word. His father worked a tower before him. And, until his father retired, then died shortly after, they carpooled.

By chance, a lieutenant walked into the observation area. His uniform was the same as mine, except his shirt was white and he was wearing one of those hats that airline pilots wear. But he looked more like a bus driver. A sloppy one that needed to shave.

Melvin was done heaving then, but still crying. I lifted him up and sat him on a clean part of his bunk. His skin was hot. The lieutenant grabbed a paper cup from the guard station, filled it with water, and told Melvin to drink.

Melvin chugged it down. And before it happened, because I knew it would, I moved back again. Melvin sprayed the water right back out with the rest of his stomach acids.

I was still not excited, but was proud. I had officially become desensitized. No, proud isn't the right word. Disturbed. No gagging, no revulsion, just annoyance. Annoyed that I had to help, that I had to work. Annoyed with Melvin. I hated him. Why did I have to watch him?

I saw myself in twenty years, detached, in a tower, sitting, letting down the rope, fishing for my lunch. I saw myself reeling up the lunch cooler, getting mad because I asked for wheat bread, not white, and then waving to my son, who had his own uniform walking him around the yard, chasing after inmates, telling them they could only play touch football, not tackle. We'd escape every night, then ride back to the jail together the next day and stand at the gate, waiting, I guess, for a paycheck.

That place, it was just ugly, filling me up. One more year and I'd be too heavy to leave. And like Melvin and his eggs, I couldn't digest them. But I couldn't spit them out either, and they curdled.

I dragged Melvin to the shower, put him inside, and pulled off his smock. He fell when I turned the water on. So I picked him up, soaking my right sleeve. I squirted him with the combination soap/shampoo. I told him he had eggs in his hair. He wiped and his curls threw bits onto my arm.

I held up that miniature naked man, that baby, who sobbed as he washed. The lieutenant said, "Eggs. I'm hungry."

Breakfast, it was my next stop.

Me too, I told the lieutenant. I'm starving.

Jail speak for deadened.

Jail speak for numb.

Jail speak for done.

When Melvin was clean, the lieutenant handed him a towel. I showered the eggs off my boots. The drain was clogged.

The inmate janitors, who made seventy-nine cents an hour minus taxes, shoveled the eggs out of Melvin's cell with dustpans. I heard them in there. "Melvin, that fuck. That fucking fuck." Melvin wasn't just notorious with the nurses. The shit painting Melvin had created, those same janitors had to wash it off.

I grabbed a clean smock. I could only find a medium so it fit like the crotch of my pants, not even close. The smock covered Melvin completely, including his size 6 feet.

I strapped him back down. He didn't fight. And for the time it took me to shut his door, lock it, wring out my sleeve, and walk back to his window, Melvin had fallen asleep. He looked comfortable and clean on his bunk—or as comfortable as you can get in five-point restraints.

Sitting next to the nurses then, holding his hat, the lieutenant said, "Good job."

I thought it probably wasn't.

Afterword

I HAVE, at times, felt slimy for telling parts of Melvin's story. It is, after all, his.

And I've struggled to come up with a lesson or solution to offer the world about him. When I think of Melvin, I think of Kurt Vonnegut, who says about war, "There is nothing intelligent to say about a massacre."

Maybe recording a few of Melvin's moments stomping around is enough.

AFTER jail I built a greenhouse. Our house in Missouri came with an old metal-sided pole barn. The inside: a horse stall and our neighbor's tractor. At some point a tree had fallen on the roof. The doors were stuck open. Wood bees, wasps, bird nests, dry rot, that was the shed.

I bought fifty storm doors from a guy who had a pile of them leaning against his house. I homeschooled my kids for a year and went to school myself. Eventually I took a few jobs, one teaching at-risk teenagers during the day, the next generation of Melvins, another teaching college at night. On the weekends I wrote and framed-in windows. I plugged the holes, wrestled with my decision to be a guard, scraped out the wasp nests, admitted to abusing my power, replaced the dry rot, decided to stop lying about my role in jail, and replaced the roof panels to let in the light.

Somewhere in there I watched a World War II film for a psychology class. The assignment: mating behaviors. But what happened was, the film ruined me for days. It was terrible. I mean, the movie was good. It won awards. It had drama and suspense and relatable characters. But it gave me a certain painful funk that I couldn't heavy-bag my way out of.

So I asked my wife to watch it. But warned her first. Then worked in the office until it was over and when I came out I saw she was crying. Sobbing even. Tissues in both hands. Curled on the couch. And right then, looking at her puffed-up eyes and wrinkled chin, that's when I identified the unknown crap feeling I had had for three days:

I was sad.

HOW wonderful it was to learn that about myself.

I finally knew what I felt when I saw the suicide victims.

And when I worked the visiting room.

And when Melvin made me laugh.

Now I walk around plenty sad all the time. And that's great. I have positive strategies to deal with it. Like a greenhouse.

I'm not saying that working inside detaches people from their emotions.

But probably it definitely does.

And the idea for the greenhouse was to build this nurturing structure to feed the family for an entire month. It'd be basic: work land, reap food. Show how much I care. I put in the last window. I wrote this afterword.

Jail ended with zero punches thrown in my direction. I made money from it—even for doing the wrong thing. I got a farewell party at the sports club from the guards. One gave me a brownie cookbook. He knew I was on my way to be a stay-at-home dad.

But I only did three years inside. That's it. Barely any time. Some guards go for thirty.

And I don't know what it means to be an inmate. Maybe I have a better idea than the general public. But nothing certain. Sometimes, they even looked happy. We joked together. We laughed. We said hi and bye and wassup to each other. But I wasn't one. So I won't say.

WE can't stop war. And we can't stop crime. But, please, let's keep the kids out of jail. Melvin's gone now. The state has little transparency when it comes to prisons and even less when it comes to state mental hospitals. I know he paroled after I left Rockview, was sent to another group home, was caught with matches and a lighter, and put back in jail. But he's not in the Pennsylvania inmate locator anymore. So that means either he changed his name. Or he's out. Or he's in another group home. Or he's in a state mental hospital. Or he's dead.

BUT when first I wrote about jail, I wrote about Melvin. So I'll leave you with this story. About halfway through my time, he was coloring in his cell. He told me, "Therapist will give me candy for it." I heard it was something about expressing his emotions. He used grease pencils, pseudo-crayons the guards used to fill out the blocks' population boards: black for black inmates, green for Hispanics, red for Caucasians. Inmates made tattoo ink out of them. Melvin drew green grass, red clouds, black-and-green trees. The birds: big curved Ms—you know the type. A red sun. And Melvin said, "Don't look. Don't look." and he leaned over to cover the page. But it was too late. I saw that it was a picture of him and the block sergeant holding hands. He was black. The sergeant was red. In Melvin's other hand he held the string of a black kite flying dangerously close to a red cloud.

THERE. That's nice, isn't it?